The Little Book
of

LOVE
POEMS

The Little Book

of

LOVE

POEMS

Edited by

ESME HAWES

SIENA

This edition published and distributed by Siena, 1998

Siena is an imprint of Parragon

Parragon
13 Whiteladies Road
Clifton
Bristol BS8 1PB

Produced by Magpie Books, an imprint of
Robinson Publishing Ltd, London

Cover illustration courtesy of Flowers & Foliage

ISBN 0 75252 687 1

A copy of the British Library Cataloguing-in-Publication Data
is available from the British Library

Contents

Introduction

Romeo and Juliet are the world's most famous lovers. Although most of our love affairs aren't quite as dramatic in outcome as theirs, we can sympathize with the classic stages of their romance since, while we all feel our affairs are uniquely intense, we also sense the universality of our emotions. Many of us try to express that feeling with some touching lines of poetry. Most of us, though good on the unique, are less successful at capturing the universal. Here is as broad a selection as possible of some of the poets who were more successful.

Chapter 1

DESIRE

ROMEO (*To a Servingman*): What lady's that which
    doth enrich the hand of yonder knight?
SERVANT: I know not, sir.
ROMEO: O! she doth teach the torches to burn
    bright.
    It seems she hangs upon the cheek of night
    Like a rich jewel in an Ethiope's ear;
    Beauty too rich for use, for earth too dear!
    So shows a snowy dove trooping with crows,
    As yonder lady o'er her fellows shows.
    The measure done, I'll watch her place of stand,
    And, touching hers, make blessed my rude hand.
    Did my heart love till now? forswear it, sight!
    For I ne'er saw true beauty till this night.

Act I Scene v

Love is Like a Dizziness

~

O, Love, love, love!
Love is like a dizziness;
It winna let a poor body
Gang about his biziness!
James Hogg 1770–1835

First Love

I ne'er was struck before that hour
With love so sudden and so sweet
Her face it bloomed like a sweet flower
And stole my heart away complete
My face turned pale a deadly pale
My legs refused to walk away
And when she looked what could I ail
My life and all seemed turned to clay

And then my blood rushed to my face
And took my eyesight quite away
The trees and bushes round the place
Seemed midnight at noon day
I could not see a single thing
Words from my eyes did start
They spoke as chords do from the string
And blood burnt round my heart

Are flowers the winter's choice
Is love's bed always snow
She seemed to hear my silent voice
Not loves appeals to know

I never saw so sweet a face
As that I stood before
My heart has left its dwelling place
And can return no more –

John Clare 1793–1864

A Red, Red Rose

~

O my Love's like a red, red rose,
That's newly sprung in June;
O my Love's like the melodie
That's sweetly play'd in tune –

As fair art thou, my bonnie lass,
So deep in love am I;
And I will love thee still, my Dear,
Till a' the seas gang dry –

Till a' the seas gang dry, my Dear,
And the rocks melt wi' the sun:
I will love thee still, my Dear,
While the sands o' life shall run –

And fare thee well, my only Love!
And fare thee well, a while!
And I will come again, my Love,
Tho' it were ten thousand mile!

Robert Burns 1759–96

from Doctor Faustus

Was this the face that launched a thousand ships?
And burnt the topless towers of Ilium?
Sweet Helen, make me immortal with a kiss:
Her lips suck forth my soul, see where it flies:
And all is dross that is not Helena:
I will be Paris, and for love of thee,
Instead of Troy shall Wertenberg be sack'd,
And I will combat with weak Menelaus,
And wear thy colours on my plumed crest:
Yea I will wound Achilles in the heel,
And then return to Helen for a kiss.
O thou art fairer than the evening air,
Clad in the beauty of a thousand stars,
Brighter art thou than flaming Jupiter,
When he appear'd to hapless Semele,
More lovely than the monarch of the sky
In wanton Arethusa's azur'd arms,
And none but thou shalt be my paramour.

Christopher Marlowe 1564–93

Sonnet from the Portuguese XIV

~

If thou must love me, let it be for nought
Except for love's sake only. Do not say
'I love her for her smile ... her look ... her way
Of speaking gently, – for a trick of thought
That falls in well with mine, and certes brought
A sense of pleasant ease on such a day' –
For these things in themselves, Beloved, may
be changed, or change for thee, – and love, so wrought
May be unwrought so. Neither love me for
Thine own dear pity's wiping my cheeks dry,
Since one might well forget to weep who bore
Thy comfort long, and lose thy love thereby.
But love me for love's sake, that evermore
Thou may'st love on through love's eternity.

Elizabeth Barrett Browning 1806–61

On Loving Once and Loving Often

~

Once loving is a gen'ral Fashion,
To nature 'tis a Tribute paid:
But, loving often shews that Passion
Despises Reason's feeble Aid.

Elizabeth Tollet 1694–1754

Song

Go, lovely rose –
Tell her that wastes her time and me,
That now she knows,
When I resemble her to thee
How sweet and fair she seems to be.

Tell her that's young,
And shuns to have her graces spied,
That hadst thou sprung
In deserts where no men abide,
Thou must have uncommended died.

Small is the worth
Of beauty from the light retired:
Bid her come forth,
Suffer herself to be desired,
And not blush so to be admired.

Then die! – that she
The common fate of all things rare
May read in thee;
How small a part of time they share
That are so wondrous sweet and fair!

Edmund Waller 1606–87

On Her Loving Two Equally

How strongly does my passion flow,
Divided equally 'twixt two?
Damon had ne'er subdued my heart,
Had not Alexis took his part
Nor could Alexis powerful prove
Without my Damon's aid, to gain my love.

When my Alexis present is,
Then I for Damon sigh and mourn;
But when Alexis I do miss,
Damon gains nothing but my scorn
But if it chance they both are by
For both alike I languish, sigh and die.

Cure then, thou mighty winged god
This restless fever in my blood;
One golden-pointed dart take back
But which, O Cupid, wilt thou take?
If Damon's, all my hopes are crossed;
Or that of my Alexis, I am lost.

Aphra Behn   1640–89

from Love at Large

Whene'er I come where ladies are,
How sad soever I was before,
Though like a ship frost-bound and far
Withheld in ice from the ocean's roar,
Third-wintered in that dreadful dock,
With stiffened cordage, sails decayed,
And crew that care for calm and shock
Alike, too dull to be dismayed,
Yet, if I come where ladies are,
How sad soever I was before,
Then is my sadness banished far,
And I am like that ship no more.

Coventry Patmore   1823–96

Upon Julia's Clothes

Whenas in silks my Julia goes,
Then, then, methinks, how sweetly flows
That liquefaction of her clothes!

Next, when I cast mine eyes and see
That brave vibration each way free,
– O how that glittering taketh me!

Robert Herrick 1591–1674

Fire Us With Ice

As Corydon went shiv'ring by,
Sylvia a Ball of Snow let fly,
Which straight a Globe of Fire became,
And put the Shepherd in a Flame;
Cupid now break thy Darts and Bow,
Sylvia can all thy Feats out-do,
Fire us with Ice, burn us with Snow.

Mary Monk 1677–1715

To My Heavenly Charmer

My poor expecting Heart beats for thy Breast,
In ev'ry pulse, and will not let me rest;
A thousand dear Desires are waking there,
Whose softness will not a Description bear,
Oh! let me pour them to thy lovely eyes,
And catch their tender meanings as they rise.
My ev'ry Feature with my Passion glows
In ev'ry thought and look it overflows.
Too noble and too strong for all Disguise,
It rushes from my love-discov'ring Eyes.
Nor Rules nor Reason can my Love restrain;
Its godlike Tide runs high in ev'ry Vein.
To the whole World my Tenderness be known,
What is the World to her, who lives for thee alone.

Martha Sansom   1690–1736

A Picture

It was in autumn that I met
Her whom I love; the sunflowers bold
Stood up like guards around her set,
And all the air with mignonette
Was warm within the garden old;
Beside her feet the marigold
Glowed star-like, and the sweet-pea sent
A sigh to follow as she went
Slowly adown the terrace; – there
I saw thee, oh my love! and thou wert fair.

She stood in the full noonday, unafraid,
As one beloved of sunlight, for awhile
She leant upon the timeworn balustrade;
The white clematis wooed her, and the clove
Hung all its burning heart upon her smile;
And on her cheek and in her eyes was love;
And on her lips that, like an opening rose,
Seemed parting some sweet secret to disclose,
The soul of all the summer lingered; – there
I saw thee, oh my love! and thou wert fair.

Dora Greenwell 1821–82

from **Hymn to Venus**

Her sparkling necklace first he laid aside,
Her bracelets next, and braided hair unty'd;
And now his busy hand her zone unbrac'd,
Which girt her radiant robe around her waist;
Her radiant robe at last aside was thrown,
Whose rosy hue with dazzling lustre shone.
The Queen of Love the youth thus disarray'd,
And on a chair of gold her vestments laid.
Anchises now (so Jove and Fate ordain'd)
The sweet extreme of ecstasy attain'd.

Homer 750 BC approx.

Oh Lift Me!

~

Oh lift me from the grass!
I die! I faint! I fail!
Let thy love and kisses rain
On my lips and eyelids pale.
My cheek is cold and white, alas!
My heart beats loud and fast: –
Oh! Press it to thine own again,
Where it will break at last.

Percy Bysshe Shelley 1792–1822

Cupid Lost

~

Late in the Forest I did Cupid See
Colde, wet, and crying he had lost his way,
And being blind was farther like to stray:
Which sight a kind compassion bred in me.

I kindly took and dried him, while that he
Poor child complain'd he starved was with stay,
And pined for want of his accustom'd play,
For none in that wild place his host would be.

I glad was of his finding, thinking sure
This service should my freedom still procure,
And in my arms I took him then unharmed.

Carrying him safe unto a myrtle bower
But in the way he made me feel his power.
Burning my heart who had him kindly warmed.

Mary Wroth 1586–1640

from Othello *Act I Scene iii*

My story being done,
She gave me for my pains a world of sighs:
She swore, in faith, 'twas strange, 'twas passing
    strange;
'twas pitiful, 'twas wondrous pitiful:
She wish'd she had not heard it, yet she wish'd
That heaven had made her such a man; she thanked
    me
And bade me, if I had a friend that loved her,
I should but teach him how to tell my story,
And that would woo her. Upon this hint I spake:
She loved me for the dangers I had passed
And I loved her that she did pity them.

William Shakespeare 1564–1616

from Hero and Leander

It lies not in our power to love or hate
For will in us is over-ruled by fate.
When two are stripped, long ere the course begin,
We wish that one should lose, the other win;
And one especially do we affect
Of two gold ingots, like in each respect.
The reason no man knows; let it suffice,
What we behold is censured by our eyes.
Where both deliberate, the love is slight;
Who ever loved, that loved not at first sight?

Christopher Marlowe 1564–93

Blest As the Immortal Gods Is He

～

Blest as the immortal gods is he,
The youth, who fondly sits by thee,
And hears and sees thee all the while
Softly speak and sweetly smile.

'Twas this deprived my soul of rest,
And raised such tumults in my breast;
For while I gazed, in transport tost,
My breath was gone, my voice was lost:

My bosom glowed; the subtle flame
Ran quick through all my vital frame,
O'er my dim eyes a darkness hung;
My ears with hollow murmurs rung.

In dewy damps my limbs were chilled;
My blood with gentle horror thrilled;
My feeble pulse forgot to play;
I fainted, sank, and died away.

Sappho 600 BC approx.

To Cupid

Child, with many a childish wile,
Timid look, and blushing smile,
Downy wings to steal thy way,
Gilded bow, and quiver gay,
Who in thy simple mien would trace
The tyrant of the human race?
Who is he whose flinty heart
Hath not felt the flying dart?
Who is he that from the wound
Hath not pain and pleasure found?
Who is he that hath not shed
Curse and blessing on thy head?

Joanna Baillie 1762–1851

from Don Juan *Canto 69*

Juan she saw and as a pretty child,
Caressed him often. Such a thing might be
Quite innocently done and harmless styled
When she had twenty years, and thirteen he;
But I am not so sure I should have smiled
When he was sixteen, Julia twenty-three.
These few short years make wondrous alterations,
Particularly amongst sunburnt nations.

George Gordon, Lord Byron   1788–1824

Sonnet 113

~

Since I left you, mine eye is in my mind,
And that which governs me to go about
Doth part his function and is partly blind,
Seems seeing, but effectually is out;
For it no form delivers to the heart
Of bird, of flower, or shape, which it doth latch:
Of his quick objects hath the mind no part.
Nor his own vision holds what it doth catch;
For if it see the rudest or gentlest sight,
The most sweet favour or deformed'st creature,
The mountain or the sea, the day or night,
The crow or dove, it shapes them to your feature:
Incapable of more, replete with you,
My most true mind thus maketh mine untrue.

William Shakespeare 1564–1616

A Moment

The clouds had made a crimson crown
Above the mountains high.
The stormy sun was going down
In a stormy sky.

Why did you let your eyes so rest on me,
And hold your breath between?
In all the ages this can never be
As if it had not been.

Mary Elizabeth Coleridge   1861–1907

The Look

Strephon kissed me in the spring,
Robin in the fall,
But Colin only looked at me
And never kissed at all.

Strephon's kiss was lost in jest,
Robin's lost in play,
But the kiss in Colin's eyes
Haunts me night and day.

Sara Teasdale 1884–1933

While I Was Hanging a Garland

~

While I was hanging a garland at her door,
(After a party), Hermonassa threw
Some water from a pot, flattening the hair
I'd curled enough to last three days or more.
And yet, the water made me hot – I knew
The pot contained her sweet lips' hidden fire.

Paulos the Silentiary   4th century BC

When I Was Young and Fair

~

When I was fair and young, then favour graced me;
Of many was I sought their mistress for to be,
But I did scorn them all, and answered them therefore:
'Go! go! go! seek some other where, importune me no
    more!'

How many weeping eyes, I made to pine with woe!
How many sighing hearts! I have no skill to show.
Yet I the prouder grew, and still this spake therefore:
'Go! go! go! seek some other where, importune me no
    more!'

Then spake fair Venus' son that proud victorious boy,
Saying: You dainty dame for that you be so coy?
I will so pluck your plumes that you shall say no more:
'Go! go! go! seek some other where, importune me no
    more!'

As soon as he had said, such change grew in my breast,
That neither night nor day, I could take any rest.
Then lo! I did repent that I had said before:
'Go! go! go! seek some other where, importune me no
    more.'

Queen Elizabeth I 1533–1603

The Knight and the Lady

The knight knocked at the castle gate;
The lady marvelled who was thereat.
To call the porter he would not blin;
The lady said he should not come in.

The portress was a lady bright;
Strangeness that lady hight.
She asked him what was his name;
He said, 'Desire, your man, Madame.'

She said, 'Desire, what do ye here?'
He said, 'Madame, as your prisoner.'
He was counselled to brief a bill,
And show my lady his own will.

'Kindness', said she, 'would it bear,'
'And Pity,' said she, 'would be there.'
Thus how they did we cannot say;
We left them there and went our way.

William Cornish d. 1524

Between Your Sheets

Between your sheets you soundly sleep
Nor dream of vigils that we lovers keep
While all the night, I waking sigh your name,
The tender sound does every nerve inflame,
Imagination shows me all your charms,
The plenteous silken hair and waxen arms,
The well turned neck and snowy rising breast
And all the beauties that supinely rest
between your sheets.

Ah Lindamira, could you see my heart,
How fond, how true, how free from fraudful art,
The warmest glances poorly do explain
The eager wish, the melting throbbing pain
Which through my very blood and soul I feel,
Which you cannot believe nor I reveal,
Which every metaphor must render less
And yet (methinks) which I could well express
between your sheets.

Lady Mary Wortley Montagu 1689–1762

from Ruth

Round her eyes her tresses fell,
Which were blackest none could tell,
But long lashes veiled a light,
That had else been all too bright.

And her hat, with shady brim,
Made her tressy forehead dim;
Thus she stood amid the stooks,
Praising God with sweetest looks: –

Sure, I said, heaven did not mean,
Where I reap thou shouldst but glean,
Lay thy sheaf adown and come,
Share my harvest and my home.

Thomas Hood 1799–1845

Sonnet

I wish I could remember that first day,
First hour, first moment of your meeting me.
If bright or dim the season, it might be
Summer or Winter for aught that I can say:
So unrecorded did it slip away,
So blind was I to see and to foresee,
So dull to mark the budding of my tree
That would not blossom yet for many a May.
If only I could recollect it, such
A day of days! I let it come and go
As traceless as a thaw of bygone snow;
It seemed to mean so little, meant so much;
If only now I could recall that touch,
First touch of hand in hand. – Did one but know!

Christina Rossetti 1830–94

from Aire and Angels

Twice or thrice had I lov'd thee,
Before I knew thy face or name;
So in a voice, so in a shapelesse flame,
Angels affect us oft, and worship'd be;
Still when, to where thou wert, I came,
Some lovely glorious nothing I did see.
But since my soule, whose child love is,
Takes limmes of flesh, and else could nothing doe,
More subtile than the parent is,
Love must not be, but take a body too,
And therefore what thou wert, and who,
I bid Love aske, and now
That it assume thy body, I allow,
And fixe it selfe in thy lip, eye, and brow.

John Donne 1572–1631

Renouncement

I must not think of thee; and, tired yet strong,
I shun the love that lurks in all delight –
The love of thee – and in the blue heaven's height,
And in the dearest passage of a song.
O just beyond the fairest thoughts that throng
This breast, the thought of thee waits, hidden yet
    bright;
But it must never, never come in sight;
I must stop short of thee the whole day long.

But when sleep comes to close each difficult day,
When night gives pause to the long watch I keep,
And all my bonds I needs must loose apart,
Must doff my will as raiment laid away, –
With the first dream that comes with the first sleep
I run, I run, I am gathered to thy heart.

Alice Meynell 1847–1922

Stanzas

Oh, come to me in dreams, my love!
I will not ask a dearer bliss;
Come with the starry beams, my love,
And press mine eyelids with thy kiss.

'Twas thus, as ancient fables tell,
Love visited a Grecian maid,
Till she disturbed the sacred spell,
And woke to find her hopes betrayed.

But gentle sleep shall veil my sight,
And Psyche's lamp shall darkling be,
When, in the visions of the night,
Thou dost renew thy vows to me.

Then come to me in dreams, my love,
I will not ask a dearer bliss;
Come with the starry beams, my love,
And press mine eyelids with thy kiss.

Mary Wollstonecraft Shelley 1797–1851

And On My Eyes Dark Sleep By Night

Come, dark-eyed Sleep, thou child of Night,
Give me thy dreams, thy lies;
Lead through the horny portal white
The pleasure day denies.

O bring the kiss I could not take
From lips that would not give;
Bring me the heart I could not break,
The bliss for which I live.

I care not if I slumber blest
By fond delusion; nay,
Put me on Phaon's lips to rest,
And cheat the cruel day!

Michael Field 1846–1914

Remedia Amoris

~

Love, and the Gout invade the idle Brain,
Bus'ness prevents the Passion and the Pain:
Ceres and Bacchus, envious of our Ease,
Blow up the Flame, and heighten the Disease.
Withdraw the Fewel and the Fire goes out;
Hard Beds and Fasting, cure both Love and Gout.

Elizabeth Thomas 1675–1731

Caelica

~

Love, the delight of all well-thinking minds;
Delight, the fruit of virtue dearly loved;
Virtue, the highest good, that reason finds;
Reason, the fire wherein men's thoughts be proved;
Are from the world by Nature's power bereft,
And in one creature, for her glory, left.

Beauty, her cover is, the eyes' true pleasure;
In honour's fame she lives, the ears' sweet music;
Excess of wonder grows from her true measure;
Her worth is passion's wound, and passion's physic;
From her true heart, clear springs of wisdom flow,
Which imaged in her words and deeds, men know.

Time fain would stay, that she might never leave her,
Place doth rejoice, that she must needs contain her,
Death craves of Heaven, that she may not bereave her,
The Heavens know their own, and do maintain her;
Delight, love, reason, virtue, let it be,
To set all women light, but only she.

Fulke Greville, Lord Brooke 1554–1628

from Urania

Did I boast of liberty?
'Twas an insolence vain
I do only look on thee
And I captive am again

Mary Wroth 1586–1640

Wild Nights – Wild Nights

Wild Nights – Wild Nights!
Were I with thee
Wild Nights should be
Our luxury!

Futile – the winds –
To a heart in port –
Done with the Compass –
Done with the Chart!

Rowing in Eden –
Ash, the Sea!
Might I but moor – Tonight –
In Thee!

Emily Dickinson   1830–86

From the Telephone

~

Out of the dark cup
Your voice broke like a flower.
It trembled, swaying on its taut stem.
The caress in its touch
Made my eyes close.
Florence Ripley Mastin late 19th century

Delight in Disorder

A sweet disorder in the dresse
Kindles in cloathes a wantonnesse:
A Lawne about the shoulders thrown
Into a fine distraction: —
An erring Lace, which here and there
Enthralls the Crimson Stomacher: —
A Cuffe neglectfull, and thereby
Ribbands to flow confusedly: —
A winning wave (deserving Note)
In the tempestuous petticote: —
A carelesse shoe-string, in whose tye
I see a wilde civility: —
Doe more bewitch me, than when Art
Is too precise in every part.

Robert Herrick 1591–1674

How Long Shall I Pine?

How long shall I pine for love?
How long shall I muse in vain?
How long like the turtle-dove
Shall I heavenly thus complain?
Shall the sails of my love stand still?
Shall the grists of my hopes be unground?
Oh fie, oh fie, oh fie,
Let the mill, let the mill go round.

John Fletcher 1579–1625

from A Prayer for Indifference

~

I ask no kind return in love,
No tempting charm to please;
Far from the heart those gifts remove,
That sighs for peace and ease;

Nor peace, nor ease, the heart can know,
That like the needle true,
Turns at the touch of joy or woe,
But, turning, trembles too.

Far as distress the soul can wound,
'Tis pain in each degree:
'Tis bliss but to a certain bound,
Beyond is agony.

Frances Greville 1724–89

All Thoughts, All Passions

~

All thoughts, all passions, all delights,
Whatever stirs this mortal frame,
All are but ministers of Love,
And feed his sacred flame.
Samuel Taylor Coleridge 1772–1834

Youth and Beauty

Thou art so fair, and young withal,
Thou kindl'st young desires in me,
Restoring life to leaves that fall,
And sight to eyes that hardly see
Half those fresh beauties bloom in thee.

Those, under sev'ral herbs and flow'rs
Disguis'd, were all Medea gave,
When she recall'd time's flying hours,
And aged Aeson from his grave,
For beauty can both kill and save.

Youth it enflames, but age it cheers,
I would go back, but not return
To twenty but to twice those years;
Not blaze, but ever constant burn,
For fear my cradle prove my urn.

Aurelian Townshend 1583–1643

Western Wind

Western Wind, when wilt thou blow,
The small rain down can rain?
Christ, if my love were in my arms
And I in my bed again!

Anon   16th Century

Song

Stephon hath Fashion, Wit and Youth,
With all things else that please;
He nothing wants but Love and Truth
To ruin me with ease:
But he is flint, and beats the Art
To kindle fierce desire;
His pow'r inflames another's heart,
Yet he ne'er feels the fire.

O! how it does my soul perplex,
When I his charms recall,
To think he shou'd despise our Sex;
Or, what's worse, love 'em all!
My wearied heart, like Noah's Dove,
In vain has sought for rest;
Finding no hope to fix my Love,
Returns into my Breast.

Elizabeth Taylor 1685–1720

An Evil Spirit

An evil spirit, your beauty haunts me still,
Wherewith (alas) I have been long possess'd,
Which ceaseth not to tempt me to each ill,
Nor gives me once, but one poor minute's rest:
In me it speaks, whether I sleep or wake,
And when by means, to drive it out I try,
With greater torments then it me doth take,
And tortures me in most extremity;
Before my face, it lays down my despairs,
And hastes me on unto a sudden death;
Now tempting me, to drown myself in tears,
And then in sighing, to give up my breath;
Thus am I still provok'd to every evil,
By this good wicked spirit, sweet angel devil.

Michael Drayton 1563–1631

The Vain Advice

Ah, gaze not on those eyes! forbear
That soft enchanting voice to hear:
Not looks of basilisks give surer death,
Nor Syrens sing with more destructive breath.

Fly, if thy freedom thoud'st maintain,
Alas! I feel th'advice is vain!
A heart whose safety but in flight does lie,
Is too far lost to have the power to fly.
Catherine Cockburn 1679–1749

On His Mistress, the Queen of Bohemia

You meaner beauties of the night,
That poorly satisfy our eyes
More by your number than your light,
You common people of the skies;
What are you when the moon shall rise?

You curious chanters of the wood,
That warble forth Dame Nature's lays,
Thinking your passions understood
By your weak accents; what's your praise,
When Philomel her voice shall raise?

You violets that first appear,
By your pure purple mantles known
Like the proud virgins of the year,
As if the spring were all your own;
What are you when the rose is blown?

So, when my mistress shall be seen
In form and beauty of her mind,
By virtue first, then choice, a Queen,
Tell me if she were not designed
Th' eclipse and glory of her kind.

Sir Henry Wotton 1568–1639

At a Dinner Party

With fruit and flowers the board is decked,
The wine and laughter flow;
I'll not complain – could one expect
So dull a world to know?

You look across the fruit and flowers,
My glance your glances find. –
It is our secret, only ours,
Since all the world is blind.

Amy Levy   1861–89

Fill Ev'ry Glass

Fill ev'ry glass, for wine inspires us,
And fires us
With courage, love and joy.
Women and wine should life employ.
Is there aught else on earth desirous?

John Gay 1685–1732

And Forgive Us Our Trespasses

How prone we are to sin, how sweet were made
The pleasures, our resistless hearts invade!
Of all my crimes, the breach of all thy laws,
Love, soft bewitching love! has been the cause:
Of all the paths that vanity has trod,
That sure will soonest be forgiven of God;
If things on earth may be to heaven resembled,
It must be love, pure, constant, undissemble:
But if to sin by chance the charmer press,
Forgive, O Lord, forgive our trespasses.

Aphra Behn 1640–89

Chapter 2

COURTSHIP

JULIET: How camest thou hither, tell me, and
      wherefore?
    The orchard walls are high and hard to climb;
    And the place death, considering who thou art,
    If any of my kinsmen find thee here.
ROMEO: With love's light wings did I o'er perch these
      walls;
    For stony limits cannot hold love out,
    And what love can do that dares love attempt;
    Therefore thy kinsmen are no stop to me.

Act II Scene ii

To Celia

Drink to me, onely, with thine eyes,
And I will pledge with mine;
Or leave a kisse but in the cup,
And I'll not look for wine.
The thirst that from the soule doth rise,
Doth aske a drink divine:
But might I of Jove's Nectar sup,
I would not change for thine.
I sent thee, late, a rosie wreath,
Not so much honoring thee,
As giving it a hope, that there
It could not withered bee.
But thou thereon did'st onely breathe,
And sent'st it backe to me:
Since when it growes, and smells, I sweare,
Not of it self, but thee.

Ben Jonson 1572–1637

Appeal

Daphnis dearest, wherefore weave me
Webs of lies lest truth should grieve me?
I could pardon much, believe me:
Dower me, Daphnis, or bereave me,
Kiss me, kill me, love me, leave me, –
Damn me, dear, but don't deceive me!

Edith Nesbit   1858–1924

I Showed Her Heights

I showed her Heights she never saw –
'Wouldst Climb' I said?
She said – 'Not so' –
'With me –' I said – With me?
I showed her Secrets – Morning's Nest –
The Rope the Nights were put across –
And now – 'Would'st have me for a Guest?'
She could not find her Yes –
And then, I brake my life – And Lo,
A Light, for her, did solemn glow,
The larger, as her face withdrew –
And could she, further, 'No'?

Emily Dickinson   1830–86

Live With Me

Live with me, and be my love,
And we will all the pleasure prove
That hills and valleys, dales and fields,
And all the craggy mountains yields.

There will we sit upon the rocks,
And see the shepherds feed their flocks
By shallow rivers, by whose falls
Melodious birds sing madrigals.

There will I make thee a bed of roses,
With a thousand fragrant posies,
A cap of flowers, and a kirtle
Embroider'd all with leaves of myrtle.

A belt of straw and ivy buds
With coral clasps and amber studs,
And if these pleasures may thee move,
Then live with me and be my love.

Anon   16th century

The Caution

Soft kisses may be innocent;
But ah! too easy maid, beware;
Tho' that is all thy kindness meant,
'Tis love's delusive, fatal snare.

Nor virgin e'er at first design'd
Thro' all the maze of love to stray;
But each new path allures her mind,
Till wandering on, she lose her way.

'Tis easy ere set out to stay;
But who the useful art can teach,
When sliding down a steepy way,
To stop, before the end we reach?

Keep ever something in thy power,
Beyond what would thy honour stain:
He will not dare to aim at more,
Who for small favours sighs in vain.

Catherine Cockburn 1679–1749

Song

〜

A Scholar first my Love implor'd,
And then an empty, titled Lord;
The Pedant talk'd in lofty Strains;
Alas! his Lordship wanted Brains;
I list'ned not, to one or t'other,
But straight referr'd them to my Mother.

A Poet next my Love assail'd,
A lawyer hop'd to have prevail'd;
The Bard too much approv'd himself,
The Lawyer thirsted after Pelf:
I not, to one or t'other,
But still referr'd them to my Mother.

An Officer my Heart would storm,
A miser, sought me too, in Form;
But Mars was over-free and bold,
The Miser's Heart was in his Gold:
I list'ned not, to one or t'other,
Referring still unto my Mother.

And after them, some twenty more,
Successless were, as those before;
When Damon, lovely Damon, came!
Our hearts strait felt a mutual Flame;
I vow'd I'd have him, and no other,
Without referring to my Mother.

Dorothea Du Bois   1728–74

A Lover's Plea

Shall I come, sweet Love, to thee,
When the evening beams are set?
Shall I not excluded be?
Will you find no feigned let?
Let me not, for pity, more
Tell the long hours at your door.

Who can tell what thief or foe
In the covert of the night
For his prey will work my woe,
Or through wicked foul despite?
So may I die unredressed,
Ere my long love be possessed.

But to let such dangers pass,
Which a lover's thoughts disdain,
'Tis enough in such a place
To attend love's joys in vain.
Do not mock me in thy bed,
While these cold nights freeze me dead.

Thomas Campion   1567–1620

To a Lady Making Love

Good madam, when ladies are willing,
A man must needs look like a fool;
For me I would not give a shilling
For one who would love out of rule.

You should leave us to guess by your blushing,
And not speak the matter so plain;
'Tis ours to write and be pushing,
'Tis yours to affect disdain.

That you're in a terrible taking,
By all these sweet oglings I see,
But the fruit that can fall without shaking,
Indeed is too mellow for me.

Lady Mary Wortley Montagu 1689–1762

O Mistress Mine, *from Twelfth Night*

O mistress mine, where are you roaming?
O stay and hear, your true love's coming,
That can sing both high and low.
Trip no further, pretty sweeting.
Journeys end in lovers meeting,
Every wise man's son doth know.
What is love? 'tis not hereafter,
Present mirth, hath present laughter:
What's to come is still unsure.
In delay there lies no plenty,
Then come kiss me, sweet and twenty:
Youth's a stuff will not endure.

William Shakespeare 1564–1616

The Willing Mistress

Amyntas led me to a Grove,
Where all the trees did shade us;
The sun it self, though it had strove,
It could not have betray'd us:
The place secur'd from humane eyes,
No other fear allows,
But when the Winds that gently rise,
Do kiss the yielding boughs.

Down there we sat upon the moss,
And did begin to play
A thousand amorous tricks, to pass
The heat of all the day.
A many kisses he did give:
And I return'd the same
Which made me willing to receive
That which I dare not name.

His charming eyes no aid requir'd
To tell their softning tale:
On her that was already fir'd,
'Twas easy to prevail.

He did but kiss and clasp me round,
And lay'd me gently on the ground;
Ah who can guess the rest?

Aphra Behn   1640–89

Meeting at Night

The grey sea and the long black land;
And the yellow half-moon large and low;
And the startled little waves that leap
In fiery ringlets from their sleep,
As I gain the cove with pushing prow,
And quench its speed in the slushy sand.

Then a mile of warm sea-scented beach;
Three fields to cross till a farm appears;
A tap at the pane, the quick sharp scratch
And blue spurt of a lighted match,
And a voice less loud, thro' its joys and fears,
Than the two hearts beating each to each!

Robert Browning 1812–89

To Anthea

Bid me to live, and I will live
Thy Protestant to be;
Or bid me love, and I will give
A loving heart to thee.

A heart as soft, a heart as kind,
A heart as sound and free
As in the whole world thou canst find,
That heart I'll give to thee.

Bid that heart stay, and it will stay
To honour thy decrees:
Or bid it languish quite away,
And 't shall do so for thee.

Bid me to weep, and I will weep
While I have eyes to see:
And, having none, yet I will keep
A heart to weep for thee.

Bid me despair and I'll despair
Under that cypress-tree:

Or bid me die, and I will dare
E'en death to die for thee.

Thou art my life, my love, my heart,
The very eyes of me:
And hast command of every part
To live and die for thee.

Robert Herrick 1591–1674

Villeggiature

My window, framed in pear-tree bloom,
White-curtained shone, and softly lighted:
So, by the pear-tree, to my room
Your ghost last night climbed uninvited.

Your solid self, long leagues away,
Deep in dull books, had hardly missed me:
And yet you found this Romeo's way,
And through the blossom climbed and kissed me.

I watched the still and dewy lawn,
The pear-tree boughs hung white above you:
I listened to you till the dawn,
And half forgot I did not love you.

Oh, dear! what pretty things you said,
What pearls of song you threaded for me!
I did not – till your ghost had fled –
Remember how you always bore me!

Edith Nesbit 1858–1924

from The Art of Coquetry

First form your artful looks with studious care,
From mild to grave, from tender to severe.
Oft on the careless youth your glances dart,
A tender meaning let each glance impart.
Whene'er he meet your looks, with modest pride
And soft confusion turn your eyes aside,
Let a soft sigh steal out, as if by chance,
Then cautious turn, and steal another glance,
Caught by these arts, with pride and hope elate,
The destined victim rushes on his fate;

Charlotte Lennox   1720–1804

I Will Not Give Thee All My Heart

I will not give thee all my heart
For that I need a place apart
To dream my dreams in and I know
Few sheltered ways for dreams to go:
But when I shut the door upon
Some secret wonder – still, withdrawn –
Why does thou love me even more,
And hold me closer than before?

When I of love demand the least,
Thou biddest him to fire and feast:
When I am hungry and would eat,
There is no bread, though crusts were sweet.
If I with manna may be fed,
Shall I go all uncomforted?
Nay! Howsoever dear thou art,
I will not give thee all my heart.

Grace Hazard Conkling late 19th century

Song

〜

Nothing ades to Loves fond fire
More than scorn and cold disdain
I to cherish your desire
Kindness used but twas in vain
You insulted on your slave
To be mine you soon refused
Hope not then the power to have
Which ingloriously you used
Think not Thersis I will ere
By my love my empire loose
You grow constant through dispare
Kindness you would soon abuse
Though you still possess my heart
Scorn and rigor I must fain
There remains no other art
Your love fond fugitive to gain.

Elizabeth Wilmot d. 1681

Enflam'd with Love

Enflam'd with love and led by blind desires,
The man persues, the blushful maid retires.
He hopes for pleasures, but she fears the pain,
His love but ignorance is, her feares more vain.
When e're he tast's those joys so pris'd before
He'll love no longer and she'll feare no more.
Charles Sackville, Earl of Dorset 1638–1706

Plain as the Glistering Planets Shine

Plain as the glistering planets shine
When winds have cleaned the skies,
Her love appeared, appealed for mine,
And wantoned in her eyes.

Clear as the shining tapers burned
On Cytherea's shrine,
Those brimming, lustrous beauties turned,
And called and conquered mine.

The beacon-lamp that Hero lit
No fairer shone on sea,
No plainlier summoned will and wit,
Than hers encouraged me.

I thrilled to feel her influence near,
I struck my flag at sight.
Her starry silence smote my ear
Like sudden drums at night.

I ran as, at the cannon's roar,
The troops the ramparts man –

As in the holy house of yore
The willing Eli ran.

Here, lady, lo! that servant stands
You picked from passing men,
And should you need not heart nor hands
He bows and goes again.

Robert Louis Stevenson   1850–94

To Cloris

~

Cloris, I cannot say your Eyes
Did my unwary Heart surprise;
Nor will I swear it was your Face,
Your Shape, or any nameless Grace:
For you are so entirely Fair
To love a Part, Injustice were,
No drowning Man can know which Drop
Of water his last Breath did stop,
So when the Stars in Heaven appear,
And join to make the Night look clear,
The light we no one's Bounty call,
But the obliging Gift of all.
He that does Lips or Hands adore
Deserves them only, and no more;
But I love All, and every Part,
And nothing less can ease my Heart.
Cupid, that Lover weakly strikes,
Who can express what 'tis he likes.

Sir Charles Sedley 1639–1701

Once We Played

Once we played at love together –
Played it smartly, if you please;
Lightly, as a windblown feather,
Did we stake a heart apiece.

Oh, it was delicious fooling!
In the hottest of the game,
Without thought of future cooling,
All too quickly burned Life's flame.

In this give-and-take of glances,
Kisses sweet as honey dews,
When we played with equal chances,
Did you win, or did I lose?

Mathilde Blind 1841–96

from Silent Is the House

Come, the wind may never again
Blow as now it blows for us;
And the stars may never again shine as now they
  shine;
Long before October returns,
Seas of blood will have parted us;
And you must crush the love in your heart, and I
  the love in mine!

Emily Brontë 1818–48

To ...

One word is too often profaned
For me to profane it;
One feeling too falsely disdained
For thee to disdain it;
One hope is too like despair
For prudence to smother;
And pity from thee more dear
Than that from another.

I can give not what men call love:
But wilt thou accept not
The worship the heart lifts above
And the heavens reject not,
The desire of the moth for the star,
Of the night for the morrow,
The devotion to something afar
From the sphere of our sorrow?

Percy Bysshe Shelley 1792–1822

Dear, Why Make You More of a Dog?

Dear, why make you more of a dog than me?
If he do love, I burn, I burn in love:
If he wait well, I never thence would move:
If he be fair, yet but a dog can be.
Little he is, so little worth is he;
He barks, my songs thine own voice oft doth prove:
Bidd'n, perhaps he fetcheth thee a glove,
But I unbid, fetch even my soul to thee.
Yet while I languish, him that bosom clips,
That lap doth lap, nay lets, in spite of spite,
This sour-breath'd mate taste of those sugar'd lips.
Alas, if you grant only such delight
To witless things, the Love I hope (since wit
Becomes a clog) will soon ease me of it.

Sir Philip Sidney 1554–86

Elegie: To His Mistris Going to Bed

Come, Madam, come, all rest my powers defy,
Until I labour, I in labour lie.
The foe oft-times, having the foe in sight,
Is tired with standing, though they never fight.
Off with that girdle, like heavens zone glistering,
But a far fairer world incompassing.
Unpin that spangled breastplate which you wear,
That th'eyes of busy fools may be stopt there.
Unlace your self, for that harmonious chime
Tells me from you that now it is bed time.
Off with that happy busk, which I envie,
That still can be, and still can stand so nigh.
Your gown going off such beauteous state reveals
As when from flow'ry meads th'hill's shadow steals.
Off with that wiry coronet and show
The hairy diadem which on you doth grow:
Now off with those shoes, and then safely tread
In this love's hallow'd temple, this soft bed.
In such white robes, heaven's angels us'd to be
Receiv'd by men; thou angel bring'st with thee
A heaven like Mahomet's paradise; and though
Ill spirits walk in white, we easily know
By this these angels from an evil sprite,

Those set our hairs, but these our flesh upright.
    License my roving hands, and let them go,
Before, behind, between, above, below.
O my America! my new-found-land,
My kingdom, safeliest when with one man mann'd,
My mine of precious stones, my emperie,
How blest am I in this discovering thee!
To enter in these bonds, is to be free;
Then where my hand is set, my seal shall be.
    Full nakedness! All joys are due to thee,
As souls unbodied, bodies uncloth'd must be,
To taste whole joys. Gems which you women use
Are like Atlanta's balls, cast in men's views,
That when a fool's eye lighteth on a gem,
His earthly soul may covet theirs, not them.
Like pictures, or like books' gay coverings made
For lay-men, are all women thus array'd;
Themselves are mystic books, which only we
(Whom their imputed grace will dignify)
Must see reveal'd. Then since that I may know,
As liberally, as to a midwife, show
Thy self: cast all, year, this white linen hence,
There is no penance due to innocence.
    To teach thee, I am naked first; why then
What need'st thou have more covering than a man.

John Donne 1572–1631

~ 92 ~

Love Me at Last

Love me at last, or if you will not,
Leave me;
Hard words could never, as these half-words,
Grieve me:
Love me at last – or leave me.

Love me at last, or let the last word uttered
Be but your own;
Love me, or leave me – as a cloud, a vapor,
Or a bird flown.
Love me at last – I am but sliding water
Over a stone.

Alice Corbin late 19th century

from Venus and Adonis

~

Now quick desire hath caught the yielding prey,
And glutton-like she feeds, yet never filleth;
Her lips are conquerors, his lips obey,
Praying what ransom the insulter willeth:
Whose vulture thought doth pitch the price so high,
That she will draw his lips' rich treasure dry.

And having felt the sweetness of the spoil,
With blindfold fury she begins to forage;
Her face doth reek and smoke, her blood doth boil,
And careless lust stirs up a desperate courage;
Planting oblivion, beating reason back,
Forgetting shame's pure blush, and honour's wrack.

Hot, faint, and weary, with her hard embracing,
Like a wild bird being tam'd with too much handling,
Or as the fleet-foot roe that's tir'd with chasing,
Or like the froward infant still'd with dandling,
He now obeys, and now no more resisteth,
While she takes all she can, not all she listeth.

William Shakespeare 1564–1616

Two in the Campagna

I wonder do you feel to-day
As I have felt, since, hand in hand,
We sat down on the grass, to stray
In spirit better through the land,
This morn of Rome and May?

For me, I touched a thought, I know,
Has tantalized me many times,
(Like turns of thread the spiders throw
Mocking across our path) for rhymes
To catch at and let go.

Help me to hold it! First it left
The yellowing fennel, run to seed
There, branching from the brickwork's cleft,
Some old tomb's ruin; yonder weed
Took up the floating weft,

Where one small orange cup amassed
Five beetles, – blind and green they grope
Among the honey-meal: and last,

Everywhere on the grassy slope
I traced it. Hold it fast!

The champaign with its endless fleece
Of feathery grasses everywhere!
Silence and passion, joy and peace,
An everlasting wash of air –
Rome's ghost since her decease.

Such life there, through such lengths of hours,
Such miracles performed in play,
Such primal naked forms of flowers,
Such letting nature have her way
While Heaven looks from its towers!

How say you? Let us, O my dove,
Let us be unashamed of soul,
As earth lies bare to heaven above!
How is it under our control
To love or not to love?

I would that you were all to me,
You that are just so much, no more.
Nor yours, nor mine, – nor slave nor free!
Where does the fault lie? What the core
O'the wound, since wound must be?

I would I could adopt your will,
See with your eyes, and set my heart
Beating by yours, and drink my fill
At your soul's springs, – your part, my part
In life, for good and ill.

No. I yearn upward, touch you close,
Then stand away. I kiss your cheek,
Catch your soul's warmth, – I pluck the rose
And love it more than tongue can speak –
Then the good minute goes.

Already how am I so far
Out of that minute? Must I go
Still like the thistle-ball, no bar,
Onward, whenever light winds blow,
Fixed by no friendly star?

Just when I seemed about to learn!
Where is the thread now? Off again!
The old trick! Only I discern –
Infinite passion, and the pain
Of finite hearts that yearn.

Robert Browning 1812–89

from A Fragment

For when in Floods of Love we're drench'd,
The Flames are by enjoyment quench'd:
But thus, let's thus together lie,
And kiss out long Eternity:
Here we dread no conscious spies,
No blushes stain our guiltless Joys:
Here no Faintness dulls Desires,
And Pleasure never flags, nor tires:
This has pleas'd, and pleases now,
And for Ages will do so:
Enjoyment here is never down,
But fresh, and always but begun.

Petronius   1st century AD

Giving

~

You think I give myself to you?
Not so, my friend, you do not see
My single purpose and intent –
To make you give myself to me.
Nora Cunningham late 19th century

The Baffled Knight

There was a knight, and he was young,
A riding along the way, sir,
And there he met a lady fair,
Among the cocks of hay, sir.

Quoth he, Shall you and I, lady,
Among the grass lye down a?
And I will have a special care
Of rumpling of your gown a.

'If you will go along with me
Unto my father's hall, sir,
You shall enjoy my maiden head,
And my estate and all, sir.'

So he mounted her on a milk-white steed,
Himself upon another,
And then they rid upon the road,
Like sister and like brother.

And when she came to her father's house,
Which was moated round about, sir,

She stepped straight within the gate,
And shut this young knight out, sir.

'Here is a purse of gold,' she said,
'Take it for your pains, sir;
And I will send my father's man
To go home with you again, sir.

'And if you meet a lady fair,
As you go thro the next town, sir,
You must not fear the dew of the grass,
Nor the rumpling of her gown, sir.

'And if you meet a lady gay,
As you go by the hill, sir,
If you will not when you may,
You shall not when you will, sir.'

Anon

The Invitation

Damon I cannot blame your will,
'Twas Chance and not Design did kill;
For whilst you did prepare your Charmes,
on purpose Silvia to subdue:
I met the Arrows as they flew,
And sav'd her from their harms

Alas she cannot make returnes,
Who for a Swaine already Burns;
A shepherd whom she does Caress
With all the softest marks of Love,
And 'tis in vain thou seek'st to move,
The cruel Shepherdess.

Content thee with this Victory,
Think me as fair and young as she:
I'le make thee garlands all the day,
And in the groves we'll sit and sing;
I'le crown thee with the pride o'th'Spring,
When thou art Lord of May.

Aphra Behn   1640–89

from Twelfth Night *Act I Scene v*

Make me a willow cabin at your gate,
And call upon my soul within the house;
Write loyal cantons of contemned love,
And sing them loud even in the dead of night;
Holla your name to the reverberate hills,
And make the babbling gossip of the air
Cry out 'Olivia!' O! you should not rest
Between the elements of air and earth,
But you should pity me!

William Shakespeare 1564–1616

Mediocrity in Love Rejected

Give me more love or more disdain;
The torrid or the frozen zone
Bring equal ease unto my pain,
The temperate affords me none:
Either extreme of love or hate,
Is sweeter than a calm estate.

Give me a storm; if it be love,
Like Danae in that golden shower,
I swim in pleasure; if it prove
Disdain, that torrent will devour
My vulture-hopes; and he's possess'd
Of heaven, that's but from hell released.
Then crown my joys or cure my pain:
Give me more love or more disdain.

Thomas Carew 1595–1639

The Pearl

I know the ways of Learning; both the head
And pipes that feed the press, and make it run;
What reason hath from nature borrowed,
Or of it self, like a good huswife, spun
In laws and policie; what the stars conspire,
What willing nature speaks, what forc'd by fire;
Both th'old discoveries, and the new-found seas,
The stock and surplus, cause and historie:
All these stand open, or I have the keys:
Yet I love thee.

I know the ways of Honour, what maintains
The quick returns of courtesie and wit:
In vies of favours whether partie gains,
When glorie swells the heart, and moldeth it
To all expressions both of hand and eye,
Which on the world a true-love-knot may tie,
And bear the bundle, wheresoe'er it goes:
How many drammes of spirit there must be
To sell my life unto my friends or foes:
Yet I love thee.

I know the ways of Pleasure, the sweet strains,
The lullings and the relishes of it;
The propositions of hot blood and brains;
What mirth and music mean; what love and wit
Have done these twenty hundred years and more:
I know the projects of unbridled store:
My stuffe is flesh, not brass, my senses live,
And grumble oft, that they have more in me
Than he that curbs them, being but one to five:
Yet I love thee.

I know all these, and have them in my hand:
Therefore not sealed, but with open eyes
I flie to thee, and fully understand
Both the main sale and the commodities;
And at what rate and price I have thy love;
With all the circumstances that may move:
Yet through these labyrinths, not my groveling wit,
But thy silk twist let down from heav'n to me,
Did both conduct and teach me, how by it
To climb to thee.

George Herbert 1593–1633

Cean Dubh Deelish

Put your head, darling, darling, darling,
Your darling black head my heart above;
Oh, mouth of honey, with the thyme for fragrance,
Who, with heart in breast, could deny you love?
Oh, many and many a young girl for me is pining,
Letting her locks of gold to the cold wind free,
For me, the foremost of our gay young fellows;
But I'd leave a hundred, pure love, for thee!
Then put your head, darling, darling, darling,
Your darling black head my heart above;
Oh, mouth of honey, with the thyme for fragrance,
Who, with heart in breast, could deny you love?

Sir Samuel Ferguson   1810–86

I'll Never Love Thee More

My dear and only love, I pray
That little world of thee
Be governed by no other sway
Than purest monarchy;
For if confusion have a part
(Which virtuous should abhor),
And hold a synod in thine heart,
I'll never love thee more.

Like Alexander I will reign,
And I will reign alone;
My thoughts did evermore disdain
A rival on my throne.
He either fears his fate too much,
Or his deserts are small,
That dares not put it to the touch,
To gain or lose it all.

And in the empire of thine heart,
Where I should solely be,
If others do pretend a part
Or dare to vie with me,

Or if Committees thou erect,
And go on such a score,
I'll laugh and sing at thy neglect,
And never love thee more.

But if thou wilt prove faithful then,
And constant of thy word,
I'll make thee glorious by my pen
And famous by my sword;
I'll serve thee in such noble ways
Was never heard before;
I'll crown and deck thee all with bays,
And love thee more and more.

James Graham, Marquis of Montrose 1612–56

To My Young Lover

Incautious Youth, why do'st thou so misplace
Thy fine encomiums on an o'er-blown Face;
Which after all the Varnish of the Quill,
Its pristine wrinkles shew apparent still:
Nor is it in the power of Youth to move
An age-chill'd heart to any strokes of Love.
Then chuse some budding Beauty, which in time
May crown thy wishes in thy blooming prime:
For nought can make a more preposterous show,
Than April's Flowers stuck on St Michael's Bow.
To consecrate thy first-born Sighs to me,
A superannuated Deity;
Makes that Idolatry and deadly sin,
Which otherwise had only venial been.

Jane Barker 1652–1727

Beauty

Let us use it while we may;
Snatch those joys that haste away.
Earth her winter-coat may cast,
And renew her beauty past;
But, our winter come, in vain
We solicit spring again:
And when our furrows snow shall cover,
Love may return, but never lover.
Sir Richard Fanshawe 1608–66
(from the Italian of Giovanni Battista Guarini)

To the Virgins, To Make Much of Time

Gather ye rose-buds while ye may,
Old Time is still a flying:
And this same flower that smiles to-day,
Tomorrow will be dying.

The glorious lamp of heaven, the Sun,
The higher he's a getting;
The sooner will his race be run,
And nearer he's to setting.

That age is best, which is the first,
When youth and blood are warmer;
But being spent, the worse, and worst
Times, still succeed the former.

Then be not coy, but use your time;
And while ye may, go marry:
For having lost but once your prime,
You may for ever tarry.

Robert Herrick 1591–1674

To Minnie

A picture-frame for you to fill,
A paltry setting for your face,
A thing that has no worth until
You lend it something of your grace,

I send (unhappy I that sing
Laid by awhile upon the shelf)
Because I would not send a thing
Less charming than you are yourself.

And happier than I, alas!
(Dumb thing, I envy its delight)
'Twill wish you well, the looking-glass,
And look you in the face to-night.

Robert Louis Stevenson   1850–94

Love's Philosophy

The fountains mingle with the river
And the rivers with the ocean,
The winds of heaven mix for ever
With a sweet emotion;
Nothing in the world is single,
All things by a law divine
In one another's being mingle –
Why not I with thine?

See the mountains kiss high heaven
And the waves clasp one another;
No sister-flower would be forgiven
If it disdain'd its brother:

And the sunlight clasps the earth,
And the moonbeams kiss the sea –
What are all these kissings worth,
If thou kiss not me?

Percy Bysshe Shelley 1792–1822

To his Coy Mistress

Had we but world enough, and time,
This coyness, Lady, were no crime.
We would sit down and think which way
To walk and pass our long love's day.
Thou by the Indian Ganges' side
Should'st rubies find: I by the tide
Of Humber would complain. I would
Love you ten years before the Flood,
And you should, if you please, refuse
Till the conversion of the Jews.
My vegetable love should grow
Vaster than empires, and more slow.
An hundred years should go to praise
Thine eyes and on thy forehead gaze;
Two hundred to adore each breast,
But thirty thousand to the rest.
An age at least to every part,
And the last age should show your heart.
For, Lady, you deserve this state,
Nor would I love at lower rate.
But at my back I always hear
Time's winged chariot hurrying near;

And yonder all before us lie
Deserts of vast eternity.
Thy beauty shall no more be found,
Nor, in my marble vault, shall sound
My echoing song: then worms shall try
That long preserved virginity,
And your quaint honour turn to dust,
And into ashes all my lust.
The grave's a fine and private place
But none, I think, do there embrace.
Now therefore, while the youthful hue
Sits on thy skin like morning dew,
And while thy willing soul transpires
At every pore with instant fires,
Now let us sport us while we may,
And now, like amorous birds of prey,
Rather at once our time devour
Than languish in his slow-chapt power.
Let us roll all our strength and all
Our sweetness up into one ball,
And tear our pleasures with rough strife
Through the iron gates of life:
Thus, though we cannot make our sun
Stand still, yet we will make him run.

Andrew Marvell 1621–78

from Don Juan *Canto 115*

And Julia sate with Juan, half embraced
And half retiring from the glowing arm,
Which trembled like the bosom where 'twas placed.
Yet still she must have thought there was no harm,
Or else 'twere easy to withdraw the waist.
But then the situation had its charm,
And then – God knows what next – I can't go on;
I'm almost sorry that I e'er begun.

George Gordon, Lord Byron 1788–1824

Come Into the Garden, Maud
from Maud; A Monodrama

~

I

Come into the garden, Maud,
For the black bat, night, has flown,
Come into the garden, Maud,
I am here at the gate alone;
And the woodbine spices are wafted abroad,
And the musk of the rose is blown.

II

For a breeze of morning moves,
And the planet of Love is on high,
Beginning to faint in the light that she loves
On a bed of daffodil sky,
To faint in the light of the sun she loves,
To faint in his light, and to die.

Alfred, Lord Tennyson   1809–92

Cashel of Munster

~

I'd wed you without herds, without money, or rich
    array,
And I'd wed you on a dewy morning at day-dawn grey;
My bitter woe it is, love, that we are not far away
In Cashel town, though the bare deal board were our
    bed this day;

Oh, fair maid, remember the green hill side,
Remember how I hunted about the valleys wide;
Time now, has worn me; my locks are turn'd to grey,
The year is scarce and I am poor, but send me not,
    love, away!

Oh, deem not my blood is of base strain, my girl,
Oh, deem not my birth was as the birth of the churl;
Marry me, and prove me, and say soon you will,
That noble blood is written on my right side still!

My purse holds no red gold, no coin of the silver
    white,
No herds are mine to drive through the long twilight!

But the pretty girl that would take me, all bare though
    I be and lone
Oh, I'd take her with me kindly to the county Tyrone.

Oh, my girl, I can see 'tis in trouble you are,
And, oh, my girl, I see 'tis your people's reproach you
    bear:
'I am a girl in trouble for his sake with whom I fly,
And, oh, may no other maiden know such reproach
    as I!'

Sir Samuel Ferguson   1810–86

Chapter 3

CONTENTMENT

ROMEO: Ah! Juliet, if the measure of thy joy
     Be heaped like mine, and that thy skill be more
     To blazon it, then sweeten with thy breath
     This neighbour air, and let rich music's tongue
     Unfold the imagined happiness that both
     Receive in either by this dear encounter.

JULIET: Conceit, more rich in matter than in words,
     Brags of his substance, not of ornament:
     They are but beggars that can count their
         worth;
     But my true love is grown to such excess
     I cannot sum up half my sum of wealth.

Act II Scene vi

One Day I Wrote Her Name

One day I wrote her name upon the strand,
But came the waves and washed it away:
Again I wrote it with a second hand,
But came the tide, and made my pains his prey.
Vain man, said she, that dost in vain assay
A mortal thing so to immortalize,
For I myself shall like to this decay,
And eke my name be wiped out likewise.
Not so, (quod I) let baser things devise
To die in dust, but you shall live by fame:
My verse your virtues rare shall eternize,
And in the heavens write your glorious name:
Where, whenas Death shall all the world subdue,
Our love shall live, and later life renew.

Edmund Spenser 1552–99

Sonnet 18

～

Shall I compare thee to a summer's day?
Thou art more lovely and more temperate:
Rough winds do shake the darling buds of May,
And summer's lease hath all too short a date:
Sometime too hot the eye of heaven shines,
And often is his gold complexion dimm'd,
And every fair from fair sometime declines,
By chance, or nature's changing course untrimm'd:
But thy eternal summer shall not fade,
Nor lose possession of that fair thou owest,
Nor shall death brag thou wandrest in his shade,
When in eternal lines to time thou growest,
So long as men can breathe, or eyes can see
So long lives this, and this gives life to thee.

William Shakespeare 1564–1616

To My Dear and Loving Husband

If ever two were one, then surely we.
If ever man were lov'd by wife, then three.
If ever wife was happy in a man,
Compare with me, ye woman, if you can.
I prize thy love more than whole mines of gold,
Or all the riches that the east doth hold.
My love is such that rivers cannot quench,
Nor ought but love from thee give recompence.
Thy love is such I can no way repay;
The heavens reward thee manifold I pray.
Then while we live, in love let's so persevere,
That when we love no more, we may live ever.

Anne Bradstreet 1612–72

The Good-Morrow

~

I wonder by my troth, what thou, and I
Did, till we lov'd? were we not wean'd till then?
But suck'd on country pleasures, childishly?
Or snorted we in the seven sleepers den?
'Twas so; But this, all pleasures fancies bee.
If ever any beauty I did see,
Which I desir'd, and got, 'twas but a dreame of thee.

And now good morrow to our waking soules,
Which watch not one another out of feare;
For love, all love of other sights controules,
And makes one little roome, an every where.
Let sea-discoverers to new worlds have gone,
Let Maps to other, worlds on worlds have showne,
Let us possesse one world, each hath one, and is one.

My face in thine eye, thine in mine appeares,
And true plaine hearts doe in the faces rest,
Where can we finde two better hemispheres
Without sharpe North, without declining West?
What ever dyes, was not mixt equally;
If our two loves be one, or, thou and I
Love so alike, that none doe slacken, none can die.

John Donne   1572–1631

Sonnet 29

When in disgrace with fortune and men's eyes,
I all alone beweep my out-cast state,
And trouble deaf heaven with my bootless cries,
And look upon myself, and curse my fate,
Wishing me like to one more rich in hope,
Featur'd like him, like him with friends possess'd,
Desiring this man's art, and that man's scope,
With what I most enjoy contented least,
Yet in these thoughts myself almost despising,
Haply I think on thee, — and then my state,
Like to the lark at break of day arising
From sullen earth, sings hymns at heaven's gate;
For thy sweet love remember'd such wealth brings
That then I scorn to change my state with kings.

William Shakespeare 1564–1616

Stanzas for Music

I speak not – I trace not – I breathe not thy name,
There is grief in the sound – there were guilt in the
    fame,
But the tear which now burns on my cheek may impart
The deep thought that dwells in that silence of heart.

Too brief for our passion, too long for our peace,
Were those hours, can their joy or their bitterness
    cease?
We repent – we abjure – we will break from our chain;
We must part – we must fly to – unite it again.

Oh! thine be the gladness and mine be the guilt,
Forgive me adored one – forsake if thou wilt;
But the heart which I bear shall expire undebased,
And man shall not break it – whatever thou mayst.

And stern to the haughty, but humble to thee,
My soul in its bitterest blackness shall be;
And our days seem as swift – and our moments more
    sweet,
With thee by my side – than the world at our feet.

One sight of thy sorrow – one look of thy love,
Shall turn me or fix, shall reward or reprove;
And the heartless may wonder at all we resign,
Thy lip shall reply not to them – but to mine.

George Gordon, Lord Byron 1788–1824

Song

Nay but you, who do not love her,
Is she not pure gold, my mistress?
Holds earth aught – speak truth – above her?
Aught like this tress, see, and this tress,
And this last fairest tress of all,
So fair, see, ere I let it fall?

Because, you spend your lives in praising;
To praise, you search the wide world over:
So, why not witness, calmly gazing,
If earth holds aught – speak truth – above her?
Above this tress, and this I touch
But cannot praise, I love so much!

Robert Browning 1812–89

Her Breast is Fit for Pearls

Her breast is fit for pearls,
But I was not a 'Diver' –
Her brow is fit for thrones
But I have not a crest.
Her heart is fit for home –
I – a sparrow – build there
Sweet of twigs and twine
My perennial nest.

Emily Dickinson 1830–86

Happy Marriage

~

Thou genius of connubial love, attend!
Let silent wonder all thy powers suspend,
Whilst to thy glory I devote my lays,
And pour forth all my grateful heart in praise.
In lifeless strains let vulgar satire tell
That marriage oft is mixed with heaven and hell,
That conjugal delight is soured with spleen,
And peace and war compose the varied scene.
My muse a truth sublimer can assert,
And sing the triumphs of a mutual heart.

Thrice happy they who through life's varied tide
With equal pace and gentle motion glide,
Whom, though the wave of fortune sinks or swells,
One reason governs and one wish impels,
Whose emulation is to love the best,
Who feels no bliss but in each other blest,
Who knows no pleasure but the joys they give,
Nor cease to love but when they cease to live.
If fate these blessings in one lot combine,
Then let th'eternal page record them mine.

Thomas Blacklock 1721–91

~ 131 ~

No Other Choice

Fain would I change that note
To which fond Love hath charmed me
Long, long to sing by rote,
Fancying that that harmed me:
Yet when this thought doth come,
'Love is the perfect sum
Of all delight,'
I have no other choice
Either for pen or voice
To sing or write.

O Love! they wrong thee much
That say thy sweet is bitter,
When thy rich fruit is such
As nothing can be sweeter.
Fair house of joy and bliss,
Where truest pleasure is,
I do adore thee:
I know thee what thou art,
I serve thee with my heart,
And fall before thee.

Anon late 16th century

The Bargain

My true love hath my heart, and I have his,
By just exchange, one for the other given
I hold his dear, and mine he cannot miss,
There never was a better bargain driven.
His heart in me keeps me and him in one,
My heart in him his thoughts and senses guides;
He loves my heart, for once it was his own,
I cherish his, because in me it bides.
His heart his wound received from my sight,
My heart was wounded with his wounded heart;
For as from me on him his hurt did light,
So still methought in me his hurt did smart.
Both equal hurt, in this change sought our bliss:
My true love hath my heart and I have his.

Sir Philip Sidney 1554–86

from Epithalamion

Now is my love all ready forth to come,
Let all the virgins therefore well await,
And ye fresh boys that tend upon her groom
Prepare yourselves; for he is coming straight.
Set all your things in seemly good array
Fit for so joyful day,
The joyfulst day that ever sun did see.
Fair Sun, shew forth thy favourable ray,
And let thy lifeful heat not fervent be
For fear of burning her sunshiny face,
Her beauty to disgrace.
O fairest Phoebus, father of the Muse,
If ever I did honour thee aright,
Or sing the thing, that mote thy mind delight,
Do not thy servant's simple boon refuse,
But let this day, let this one day be mine,
Let all the rest be thine.
Then I thy sovereign praises loud will sing,
That all the woods shall answer and their echo ring.

Edmund Spenser 1552–99

The Summer

The Summer hath his joys,
And Winter his delights.
Though Love and all his pleasures are but toys,
They shorten tedious nights.

Thomas Campion 1567–1620

from My Beloved Is Mine and I Am His

Nor Time, nor Place, nor Chance, nor Death can bow
My least desires unto the least remove;
He's firmly mine by Oath; I, His, by Vow;
He's mine by Faith, and I am His by Love;
He's mine by Water; I am His by Wine;
Thus I my Best-Beloved's am; thus He is mine.

He is my Altar; I, his Holy Place;
I am his Guest; and he, my living Food;
I'm his, by Penitence; He, mine by Grace;
I'm his, by Purchase; He is mine, by Blood;
He's my supporting Elm, and I, his Vine:
Thus I my Best-Beloved's am; thus He is mine.

He gives me wealth, I give him all my Vowes:
I give him songs; He gives me length of dayes:
With wreathes of Grace he crownes my conqu'ring
     brow
And I his Temples, with a Crowne of Praise,
Which he accepts as an ev'rlasting signe,
That I my Best-Beloved's am; that He is mine.

Francis Quarles 1592–1644

A Ruddy Drop

A ruddy drop of manly blood
The surging sea outweighs;
The world uncertain comes and goes,
The lover rooted stays.

Ralph Waldo Emerson 1803–82

Sonnet 130

My mistress' eyes are nothing like the sun;
Coral is far more red than her lips' red:
If snow be white, why then her breasts are dun;
If hairs be wires, black wires grow on her head.
I have seen roses damask'd, red and white,
But no such roses see I in her cheeks;
And in some perfumes is there more delight
Than in the breath that from my mistress reeks.
I love to hear her speak, yet well I know
That music hath a far more pleasing sound:
I grant I never saw a goddess go, –
My mistress, when she walks, treads on the ground:
And yet, by heaven, I think my love as rare
As any she belied with false compare.

William Shakespeare 1564–1616

Marriage Morning

Light, so low upon earth,
You send a flash to the sun.
Here is the golden close of love,
All my wooing is done.
Oh, the woods and the meadows,
Woods where we hid from the wet,
Stiles where we stay'd to be kind,
Meadows in which we met!

Light, so low in the vale
You flash and lighten afar,
For this is the golden morning of love,
And you are his morning star.
Flash, I am coming, I come,
By meadow and stile and wood,
Oh, lighten into my eyes and heart,
Into my heart and my blood!

Heart, are you great enough
For a love that never tires?
O heart, are you great enough for love?
I have heard of thorns and briers.

Over the thorns and briers,
Over the meadows and stiles,
Over the world to the end of it
Flash for a million miles.

Alfred, Lord Tennyson   1809–92

Over the Hills and Far Away

～

MACHEATH: Were I laid on Greenland's coast,
  And in my arms embraced my lass,
  Warm amidst eternal frost,
  Too soon the half-year's night would pass.
POLLY: Were I sold on Indian soil,
  Soon as the burning day was closed,
  I could mock the sultry toil
  When on my charmer's breast reposed.
MACHEATH: And I would love you all the day,
POLLY: Every night would kiss and play,
MACHEATH: If with me you'd fondly stray
POLLY: Over the hills and far away.

John Gay 1685–1732

My Sweet Lesbia

My sweetest Lesbia, let us live and love;
And, though the sager sort our deeds reprove,
Let us not weigh them: Heaven's great lamps do dive
Into their west, and straight again revive,
But, soon as once set is our little light,
Then must we sleep one ever-during night.

If all would lead their lives in love like me,
Then bloody swords and armour should not be;
No drum nor trumpet peaceful sleeps should move,
Unless alarm came from the camp of love.
But fools do live, and waste their little light,
And seek with pain their ever-during night.

When timely death my life and fortune ends,
Let not my hearse be vex'd with mourning friends,
But let all love, rich in triumph, come,
And with sweet pastimes grace my happy tomb;
And, Lesbia, close up thou my little light,
And crown with love my ever-during night.

Thomas Campion   1567–1620

A Lynmouth Widow

~

He was straight and strong, and his eyes were blue
As the summer meeting of sky and sea,
And the ruddy cliffs had a colde hue
Than flushed his cheek when he married me.

We passed the porch where the swallows bred,
We left the little brown church behind,
And I leaned on his arm, though I had no need
Only to feel him so strong and kind.

One thing I never can quite forget;
It grips my throat when I try to pray –
The keen salt smell of a drying net
That hung on the churchyard wall that day.

He would have taken a long, long grave –
A long, long grave for he stood so tall …
Oh, God, the crash of a breaking wave,
And the smell of the nets on the churchyard wall!

Amelia Josephine Burr late 19th century

A Birthday

My heart is like a singing bird
Whose nest is in a watered shoot;
My heart is like a rainbow shell
That paddles in a halcyon sea;
My heart is gladder than all these
Because my love is come to me.

Raise me a dais of silk and down;
Hang it with vair and purple dyes;
Carve it in doves and pomegranates
And peacocks with a hundred eyes;
Work it in gold and silver grapes,
In leaves and silver fleurs-de-lys;
Because the birthday of my life
Is come, my love is come to me.

Christina Rossetti 1830–94

Sally in Our Alley

Of all the girls that are so smart
There's none like pretty Sally;
She is the darling of my heart,
And she lives in our alley.
There is no lady in the land
Is half so sweet as Sally;
She is the darling of my heart,
And she lives in our alley.

Her father he makes cabbage-nets,
And through the streets does cry 'em;
Her mother she sells laces long
To such as please to buy 'em:
But sure such folks could ne'er beget
So sweet a girl as Sally!
She is the darling of my heart,
And she lives in our alley.

When she is by, I leave my work,
I love her so sincerely;
My master comes like any Turk,
And bangs me most severely:

But let him bang his bellyful,
I'll bear it all for Sally;
She is the darling of my heart,
And she lives in our alley.

Of all the days that's in the week
I dearly love but one day –
And that's the day that comes betwixt
A Saturday and Monday;
For then I'm drest all in my best
To walk abroad with Sally;
She is the darling of my heart,
And she lives in our alley.

My master carries me to church,
And often am I blamed
Because I leave him in the lurch
As soon as text is named;
I leave the church in sermon-time
And slink away to Sally;
She is the darling of my heart,
And she lives in our alley.

When Christmas comes about again,
O, then I shall have money;

I'll hoard it up, and box and all
I'll give it to my honey:
And would it were ten thousand pounds,
I'd give it all to Sally,
She is the darling of my heart,
And she lives in our alley.

My master and the neighbours all,
Make game of me and Sally,
And, but for her, I'd better be
A slave and row a galley;
But when my seven long years are out,
O, then I'll marry Sally;
O, then we'll wed, and we'll bed –
But not in our alley!

Henry Carey c. 1687–1743

Advice to Her Son on Marriage

~

When you gain her Affection, take care to preserve it;
Lest others persuade her, you do not deserve it.
Still study to heighten the joys of her life;
Nor treat her the worse, for her being your wife.
If in judgement she errs, set her right, without pride;
'Tis the province of insolent fools to deride.
A husband's first praise, is a friend and protector:
Then change not these titles for tyrant and Hector.
Let your person be neat, unaffectedly clean,
Tho alone with your wife the whole Day you remain.
Chuse books for her study to fashion her mind,
To emulate those who excell'd of her kind.
Be religion the principal care of your life,
As you hope to be blest in your Children and Wife:
So you, in your marriage, shall gain its true End;
And find, in your Wife, a Companion and Friend.

Mary Barber 1690–1757

Those Who Love

Those who love the most,
Do not talk of their love,
Francesca, Guinevere,
Deirdre, Iseult, Heloise,
In the fragrant gardens of heaven
Are silent, or speak if at all
Of fragile inconsequent things.

And a woman used to know
Who loved one man from her youth,
Against the strength of the fates
Fighting in somber pride
Never spoke of this thing,
But hearing his name by chance,
A light would pass over her face.

Sara Teasdale   1884–1933

Lovesight

When do I see the most, beloved one?
When in the light the spirits of mine eyes
Before thy face, their altar, solemnize
The worship of that Love through thee made known?
Or when in the dusk hours, (we two alone,)
Close-kissed and eloquent of still replies
Thy twilight-hidden glimmering visage lies,
And my soul only sees thy soul its own?

O love, my love! if I no more should see
Thyself, nor on the earth the shadow of thee,
Nor image of thine eyes in any spring, –
How then should sound upon Life's darkening slope
The ground-whirl of the perished leaves of Hope,
The wind of Death's imperishable wing?

Dante Gabriel Rossetti 1828–82

Second Thoughts

I thought of leaving her for a day
In town, it was such iron winter
At Durdans, the garden frosty clay,
The woods as dry as any splinter,
The sky congested. I would break
From the deep, lethargic country air
To the shining lamps, to the clash of the play,
And to-morrow, wake
Beside her, a thousand things to say.
I planned – O more – I had almost started; –
I lifted her face in my hands to kiss, –
A face in a border of fox's fur,
For the bitter black wind had stricken her,
And she wore it – her soft hair straying out
Where it buttoned against the gray, leather snout;
In an instant we should have parted;
But at sight of the delicate world within
That fox-fur collar, from brow to chin,
At sight of those wonderful eyes from the mine,
Coal pupils, an iris of glittering spa,
And the wild, ironic, defiant shine
As of a creature behind a bar

One has captured, and, when three lives are past,
May hope to reach the heart of at last,
All that, and the love at her lips, combined
To shew me what folly it were to miss
A face with such thousand things to say,
And beside these, such thousand more to spare,
For the shining lamps, for the clash of the play –
O madness; not for a single day
Could I leave her! I stayed behind.

Michael Field 1846–1914

A Letter to Daphnis

This to the crown and blessing of my life,
The much loved husband of a happy wife;
To him whose constant passion found the art
To win a stubborn and ungrateful heart,
And to the world by tenderest proof discovers
They err, who say that husbands can't be lovers.
With such return of passion as is due,
Daphnis I love, Daphnis my thoughts pursue;
Daphnis my hopes and joys are bounded all in you.
Even I, for Daphnis' and my promise' sake,
What I in women censure, undertake.
But this from love, not vanity, proceeds;
You know who writes, and I who 'tis that reads.
Judge not my passion by my want of skill:
Many love well, though they express it ill;
And I your censure could with pleasure bear,
Would you but soon return, and speak it here.

Ann Finch 1661–1720

Speechless

Upon the marriage of two deaf and dumb persons

~

Their lips upon each other's lips are laid;
Strong moans of joy, wild laughter, and short cries
Seem uttered in the passion of their eyes.
He sees her body fair and fallen head,
And she the face whereon her soul is fed;
And by the way her white breasts sink and rise
He knows she must be shaken by sweet sighs;
But all delight of sound for them is dead.
They dance a strange, weird measure, who know not
The tune to which their dancing feet are led;
Their breath in kissing is made doubly hot
With flame of pent-up speech; strange light is shed
About their spirits, as they mix and meet
In passion-lighted silence, 'tranced and sweet.

Philip Bourke Marston   1850–87

To My Excellent Lucasia

I did not live until this time
Crown'd my felicity,
When I could say without a crime,
I am not thine, but Thee.

This carcass breath'd, and walkt, and slept,
So that the World Believ'd
There was a soul the motions kept;
But they were all deceiv'd.

For as a watch by art is wound
To motion, such was mine:
But never had Orinda found
A soul till she found thine;

Which now inspires, cures, and supplies,
And guides my darkened breast:
For thou art all that I can prize,
My joy, my Life, my Rest.

No bridegroom's nor crown-conqueror's mirth
To mine compared can be:

They have but pieces of the earth,
I've all the World in thee.

Then let our flames still light and shine,
And no false fear control,
As innocent as our design,
Immortal as our soul.

Katherine Philips 1632–64

On Marriage *from* The Prophet

~

Then Almitra spoke again and said, And what of
   Marriage, master?

And he answered saying:
You were born together, and together you shall be for
   evermore.
You shall be together when the white wings of death
   scatter your days.
Ay, you shall be together even in the silent memory of
   God.
But let there be spaces in your togetherness,
And let the winds of the heavens dance between you.

Love one another, but make not a bond of love:
Let it rather be a moving sea between the shores of
   your souls.
Fill each other's cup but drink not from one cup.
Give one another of your bread but eat not from the
   same loaf.
Sing and dance together and be joyous, but let each
   one of you be alone.
Even as the strings of a lute are alone though they
   quiver with the same music.

Give your hearts, but not into each other's keeping.
For only the hand of Life can contain your hearts.
And stand together yet not too near together:
For the pillars of the temple stand apart,
And the oak tree and the cypress grow not in each
    other's shadow.

Kahlil Gibran 1883–1931

To Celia

Not, Celia, that I juster am
Or better than the rest!
For I would change each hour, like them,
Were not my heart at rest.

But I am tied to very thee
By every thought I have;
Thy face I only care to see,
Thy heart I only crave.

All that in woman is adored
In thy dear self I find –
For the whole sex can but afford
The handsome and the kind.

Why then should I seek further store,
And still make love anew?
When change itself can give no more,
'Tis easy to be true!

Sir Charles Sedley 1639–1701

from O Lay Thy Hand in Mine

O lay thy hand in mine, dear!
We're growing old, we're growing old;
But Time hath brought no sign, dear,
That hearts grow cold, that hearts grow cold.
'Tis long, long since our new love
Made life divine, made life divine;
But age enricheth true love,
Like noble wine, like noble wine.

Gerald Massey   1828–1907

A Song

Love, thou art best of Human Joys,
Our chiefest Happiness below;
All other Pleasures are but Toys,
Music without Thee is but Noise,
And beauty but an empty show.

Heav'n, who knew best what Man wou'd move,
And raise his Thoughts above the Brute;
Said, Let him Be, and Let him Love;
That must alone his Soul improve,
Howe'er Philosophers dispute.

Ann Finch 1661–1720

Sonnet 116

~

Let me not to the marriage of true minds
Admit impediments. Love is not love
Which alters when it alteration finds,
Or bends with the remover to remove:
O, no, it is an ever-fixed mark,
That looks on tempests and is never shaken;
It is the star to every wandering bark,
Whose worth's unknown, although his height be
    taken.
Love's not Time's fool, though rosy lips and cheeks
Within his bending sickle's compass come;
Love alters not with his brief hours and weeks,
But bears it out even to the edge of doom.
If this be error and upon me proved,
I never writ, nor no man ever loved.

William Shakespeare 1564–1616

True Love

True Love is but a humble,
low-born thing,
And hath its food served up in
earthen ware:

It is a thing to walk with,
hand in hand,
Through the everydayness of
this workday world.

J. R. Lowell 1819–91

from Enough

~

Yet now, O Love, that you
Have kissed my forehead, I
Have sung indeed, can die,
And be forgotten too.

Digby Mackworth Dolben   1848–67

Last Sonnet

Bright Star! would I were steadfast as thou art –
Not in lone splendour hung aloft the night,
And watching, with eternal lids apart,
Like Nature's patient sleepless Eremite,
The moving waters at their priestlike task
Of pure ablution round earth's human shores,
Or gazing on the new soft-fallen mask
Of snow upon the mountains and the moors –
No – yet still steadfast, still unchangeable,
Pillow'd upon my fair love's ripening breast
To feel for ever its soft fall and swell,
Awake for ever in a sweet unrest;
Still, still to hear her tender-taken breath,
And so live ever – or else swoon to death.

John Keats 1795–1821

The Constant Lover

Out upon it, I have loved
Three whole days together!
And am like to love three more,
If it hold fair weather.

Time shall moult away his wings
Ere he shall discover
In the whole wide world again
Such a constant lover.

But a pox upon't, no praise
There is due at all to me:
Love with me had made no stay,
Had it been any but she.

Had it any been but she,
And that very very face,
There had been at least ere this
A dozen dozen in her place.

Sir John Suckling   1609–41

Sonnet from the Portuguese XLIII

How do I love thee? Let me count the ways.
I love thee to the depth and breadth and height
My soul can reach, when feeling out of sight
For the ends of Being and ideal Grace.
I love thee to the level of everyday's
Most quiet need, by sun and candlelight.
I love thee freely, as men strive for Right;
I love thee purely, as they turn from Praise.
I love thee with the passion put to use
In my old griefs, and with my childhood's faith.
I love thee with a love I seemed to lose
With my lost saints, – I love thee with the breath,
Smiles, tears, of all my life! – and, if God choose,
I shall but love thee better after death.
                    Elizabeth Barrett Browning 1806–61

To Fanny Brawne

This living hand, now warm and capable
Of earnest grasping, would , if it were cold
And in the icy silence of the tomb,
So haunt thy days and chill thy dreaming nights
That thou wouldst wish thine own heart dry of blood
So in my veins red life might stream again,
And thou be conscience-calmed – see here it is –
I hold it towards you.

John Keats 1795– 1821

from By the Fireside

~

My perfect wife, my Leonor,
Oh, heart my own, oh eyes, mine too,
Whom else could I dare look backward for,
With whom beside should I dare pursue
The path grey heads abhor?

Robert Browning   1812–89

Chapter 4

LOSS

ROMEO: 'Tis torture, and not mercy: heaven is here
     Where Juliet lives, and every cat and dog
     And little mouse, every unworthy thing,
     Live here in heaven and may look on her;
     But Romeo may not; more validity,
     More honourable state, more courtship lives
     In carrion flies than Romeo: they may seize
     On the white wonder of dear Juliet's hand
     And steal immortal blessing from her lips,
     Who, even in pure and vestal modesty,
     Still blush, as thinking their own kisses sin.

Act III Scene iii

La Belle Dame Sans Merci

O what can ail thee, knight-at-arms,
Alone and palely loitering?
The sedge has withered from the lake,
And no birds sing.

O what can ail thee, knight-at-arms,
So haggard and so woe-begone?
The squirrel's granary is full,
And the harvest's done.

I see a lily on thy brow
With anguish moist and fever-dew;
And on thy cheek a fading rose
Fast withereth too.

I met a lady in the meads,
Full beautiful – a faery's child,
Her hair was long, her foot was light,
And her eyes were wild.

I made a garland for her head,
And bracelets too, and fragrant zone;

She looked at me as she did love,
And made sweet moan.

I set her on my pacing steed
And nothing else saw all day long,
For sidelong would she bend, and sing
A faery's song.

She found me roots of relish sweet,
And honey wild and manna dew,
And sure in language strange she said –
'I love thee true'.

She took me to her elfin grot,
And there she wept and sigh'd full sore,
And there I shut her wild, wild eyes
With kisses four.

And there she lulled me asleep,
And there I dream'd – Ah! woe betide!
The latest dream I ever dream'd
On the cold hill side.

I saw pale kings and princes too,
Pale warriors, death-pale were they all;

They cried – 'La Belle Dame sans Merci
Hath thee in thrall!'

I saw their starved lips in the gloam
With horrid warning gaped wide,
And I awoke and found me here
On the cold hill's side.

And this is why I sojourn here
Alone and palely loitering,
Though the sedge is withered from the lake,
And no birds sing.

John Keats 1795–1821

If This Be Love

~

If this be love, to draw a weary breath,
To paint on floods till the shore cry to th'air;
With downward looks, still reading on the earth
The sad memorials of my love's despair:
If this be love, to war against my soul,
Lie down to wail, rise up to sigh and grieve,
The never-resting stone of care to roll,
Still to complain my griefs whilst none relieve.

If this be love, to clothe me with dark thoughts,
Haunting untrodden paths to wail apart;
My pleasures horror, music tragic notes,
Tears in mine eyes and sorrow at my heart.
If this be love, to live a living death,
Then do I love and draw this weary breath.

Samuel Daniel 1562–1619

I Would Not Feign a Single Sigh

I would not feign a single sigh
Nor weep a single tear for thee,
The soul within these orbs burns dry,
A desert spreads where love should be.
I would not be a worm to crawl
A wreathing suppliant in thy way;
For love is life, is heaven, and all
The beams of an immortal day.

For sighs are idle things, and vain,
And tears for idiots vainly fall,
I would not kiss thy face again
Nor round thy shining slippers crawl.
Love is the honey, not the bee,
Nor would I turn its sweets to gall
For all the beauty found in thee,
Thy lily neck, rose cheek, and all.

I would not feign a single tale
Thy kindness or thy love to seek.
Nor sigh for Jenny of the Vale,
Her ruby smile or rosy cheek.

I would not have a pain to own
For those dark curls, and those bright eyes.
A frowning lip, a heart of stone,
False love and folly I despise.

John Clare 1793–1864

To My Inconstant Mistress

When thou, poor excommunicate
From all the joys of love, shalt see
The full reward and glorious fate
Which my strong faith shall purchase me,
Then curse thine own inconstancy.

A fairer hand than thine, shall cure
That heart, which thy false oaths did wound;
And to my soul, a soul more pure
Than thine, shall by Loves hand be bound,
And both with equal glory crown'd.

Then shalt thou weepe, entreat, complain
To Love, as I did once to thee;
When all thy tears shall be as vain
As mine were then, for thou shalt be
Damn'd for thy false Apostasie.

Thomas Carew 1595–1639

Loving in Truth

Loving in truth, and fain in verse my love to show,
That she, dear she, might take some pleasure of my
    pain:
Pleasure might cause her read, reading might make
    her know,
Knowledge might pity win, and pity grace obtain,
I sought fit words to paint the blackest face of woe,
Studying inventions fine, her wits to entertain:
Oft turning others' leaves to see if thence would flow
Some fresh and fruitful showers upon my sun-burn'd
    brain.
But words came halting forth, wanting Invention's
    stay,
Invention, Nature's child, fled step-dame Study's
    blows,
And others' feet still seem'd but strangers in my way.
Thus great with child to speak, and helpless in my
    throes,
Biting my trewand pen, beating myself for spite,
Fool, said my Muse to me, look in thy heart and write.

Sir Philip Sidney 1554–86

You Smiled, You Spoke

You smiled, you spoke, and I believed,
By every word and smile deceived.
Another man would hope no more;
Nor hope what I hoped before:
But let not this last wish be vain;
Deceive, deceive me once again!

      Walter Savage Landor 1775–1864

Song

Fire, fire,
Is there no help for thy desire?
Are tears all spent? is Humber low?
Doth Trent stand still? doth Thames not flow?
And does the Ocean backward go?
Though all these can't thy fever cure,
Yet Tyburn is a cooler lure,
And since thou can'st not quench thy fire,
Go hang thy self, and thy desire.

Henry Bold 1627–83

Shall I Abide

Shall I abide this jesting?
I weep, and she's a-feasting.
O cruel fancy that so doth blind thee
To love one doth not mind thee.

Can I abide this prancing?
I weep, and she's a-dancing.
O cruel fancy so to betray me,
Thou goest about to slay me.

Anon

A Song

Absent from thee, I languish still;
Then ask me not, when I return?
The straying fool 'twill plainly kill
To wish all day, all night to mourn.

Dear! from thine arms then let me fly,
That my fantastic mind may prove
The torments it deserves to try
That tears my fixed heart from my love.

When, wearied with a world of woe,
To thy safe bosom I retire
Where love and peace and truth does flow,
May I contented there expire,

Lest, once more wandering from that heaven,
I fall on some base heart unblest,
Faithless to thee, false, unforgiven,
And lose my everlasting rest.

John Wilmot, Earl of Rochester 1647–80

My Flocks Feed Not

~

My flocks feed not,
My ewes breed not,
My rams speed not,
All is amiss.
Love is dying,
Faith's defying,
Heart's denying,
Cause of this.

Richard Barnfield 1574–1627

The Slight

~

I did but crave that I might kiss
If not her lip, at least her hand,
The coolest Lover's frequent bliss,
And rude is she that will withstand
That inoffensive libertie;
She (would you think it?) in a fume
Turn'd her about and left the room,
Not she, she vow'd, not she.

Well Chariessa then said I,
If it must thus for ever be,
I can renounce my slavery,
And since you will not, can be free:
Many a time she made me dye,
Yet (would you think't?) I lov'd the more,
But I'le not tak't as heretofore,
Not I, I'le vow, not I.

Thomas Flatman   1635–88

R. Alcona to J. Brenzaida

~

Cold in the earth, and the deep snow piled above
    thee!
Far, far removed, cold in the dreary grave!
Have I forgot, my Only Love, to love thee,
Severed at last by Time's all-wearing wave?

Now, when alone, do my thoughts no longer hover
Over the mountains on Angora's shore;
Resting their wings where heath and fern-leaves
    cover
That noble heart for ever, ever more?

Cold in the earth, and fifteen wild Decembers
From those brown hills have melted into spring –
Faithful indeed is the spirit that remembers
After such years of change and suffering!

Sweet Love of youth, forgive if I forget thee
While the World's tide is bearing me along:
Sterner desires and darker hopes beset me,
Hopes which obscure but cannot do thee wrong.

No other sun has lightened up my heaven;
No other Star has ever shone for me:
All my life's bliss from thy dear life was given –
All my life's bliss is in the grave with thee.

But when the days of golden dreams had perished
And even Despair was powerless to destroy,
Then did I learn how existence could be cherished,
Strengthened and fed without the aid of joy;

Then did I check the tears of useless passion,
Weaned my young soul from yearning after thine;
Sternly denied its burning wish to hasten
Down to that tomb already more than mine!

And even yet, I dare not let it languish,
Dare not indulge in Memory's rapturous pain;
Once drinking deep of that divinest anguish,
How could I seek the empty world again?

Emily Brontë 1818–48

Song

~

Why so pale and wan fond Lover?
Prithee why so pale?
Will, when looking well can't move her,
Looking ill prevaile?
Prithee why so pale?

Why so dull and mute young Sinner?
Prithee why so mute?
Will, when speaking well can't win her,
Saying nothing doo't?
Prithee why so mute?

Quit, quit, for shame, this will not move,
This will not take her;
If of her self she will not Love,
Nothing can make her:
The Devil take her.

Sir John Suckling   1609–41

The Lost Love

~

She dwelt among the untrodden ways
Beside the springs of Dove;
A maid whom there were none to praise
And very few to love:

A violet by a mossy stone
Half-hidden from the eye!
– Fair as a star, when only one
Is shining in the sky.

She lived unknown, and few could know
When Lucy ceased to be;
But she is in her grave, and, oh,
The difference to me!

William Wordsworth 1770–1850

How Happy a Thing

How happy a thing were a wedding
And a bedding
If a man might purchase a wife
For a twelve month and a day;
But to live with her all a man's life,
For ever and for ay,
'Till she grow as grey as a cat,
Good faith, Mr Parson, I thank you for that.

Thomas Flatman   1635–88

I Hold It True *from* In Memoriam

I hold it true, whate'er befall;
I feel it, when I sorrow most;
'Tis better to have loved and lost
Than never to have loved at all.

Alfred, Lord Tennyson 1809–92

So, We'll Go No More A-Roving

So, we'll go no more a-roving
So late into the night,
Though the heart be still as loving,
And the moon be still as bright.

For the sword outwears its sheath,
And the soul wears out the breast,
And the heart must pause to breathe,
And love itself have rest.

Though the night was made for loving,
And the day returns too soon,
Yet we'll go no more a-roving
By the light of the moon.

George Gordon, Lord Byron 1788–1824

Never Seek to Tell Thy Love

Never seek to tell thy love,
Love that never told can be;
For the gentle wind does move
Silently, invisibly.

I told my love, I told my love.
I told her all my heart,
Trembling, cold, in ghastly fears –
Ah, she doth depart.

Soon as she was gone from me
A traveller came by
Silently, invisibly –
He took her with a sigh. O, was no deny.

William Blake 1757–1827

Love's Farewell

~

Since there's no helpe, come let us kisse and part,
Nay, I have done: you get no more of me,
And I am glad, yea, glad with all my heart,
That thus so cleanly, I my selfe can free,
Shake hands for ever, cancell all our vows,
And when we meet at any time againe,
Be it not seene in either of our browes,
That we one jot of former love reteyne;
Now at the last gaspe, of love's latest breath,
When his pulse fayling, passion speechlesse lies,
When faith is kneeling by his bed of death,
And innocence is closing up his eyes,

Now if thou would'st, when all have given him over,
From death to life thou might'st him yet recover.

Michael Drayton 1563–1631

The Secret

I loved thee, though I told thee not,
Right earlily and long,
Thou wert my joy in every spot,
My theme in every song.

And when I saw a stranger face
Where beauty held the claim,
I gave it like a secret grace
The being of thy name.

And all the charms of face or voice
Which I in others see
Are but the recollected choice
Of what I felt for thee.

John Clare   1793–1864

My Picture Left in Scotland

I now thinke, Love is rather deaf, than blind
For else it could not be,
That she,
Whom I adore so much, should so slight me,
And cast my love behind:
I'm sure my language to her, was as sweet,
And every close did meet
In sentence, of as subtile feet
As hath the youngest he,
That sits in shadow of Apollo's tree.

Oh, but my conscious fears,
That flie my thoughts between,
Tell me that she hath seen
My hundreds of gray hairs,
Told seven and fortie years,
Read so much waist, as she cannot imbrace
My mountain belly, and my rockie face,
And all these through her eyes, have stopt her eares.

Ben Jonson 1572–1637

from The Lord of the Isles

~

No! sum thine Edith's wretched lot
In these brief words. He loves her not.

Sir Walter Scott 1771–1832

To J.G. on News of His Marriage

My Love? alas! I must not call you Mine,
But to your envy'd Bride that Name resign:
I must forget your lovely melting Charms,
And be forever Banisht from your Arms:
For ever? oh! the Horror of that Sound!
It gives my bleeding Heart a deadly wound:
While I might hope, although my Hope was vain,
It gave some Ease to my unpitty'd Pain,
But now your Hymen doth all Hope exclude,
And but to think is Sin, yet you intrude
On every thought; if I but close my Eyes,
Methinks your pleasing Form besides me lies;
With every Sigh I gently breathe your name,
Yet no ill thoughts pollute my hallow'd Flame;
'Tis pure and harmless, as a Lambent Fire,
And never mingled with a warm Desire:
All I have now to ask of Bounteous Heaven,
Is, that your perjuries may be forgiven:
That she who you have with your Nuptials Blest,
As She's the Happiest Wife, may prove the best:
That all our Joys may light on you alone.

Then I can be contented to have none:
And never wish that you shoul'd kinder be,
Than now and then, to cast a Thought on Me:
And, Madam, though the Conquest you have won,
Over my Strephon, has my hopes undone:
I'le daily beg of Heaven, he may be
Kinder to You, than he has been to Me.

Ephelia 1678–82

Sonnet 87

Farewell! thou art too dear for my possessing,
And like enough thou know'st thy estimate:
The charter of thy worth gives thee releasing;
My bonds in thee are all determinate.
For how do I hold thee but by thy granting?
And for that riches where is my deserving?
The cause of this fair gift in me is wanting,
And so my patent back again is swerving.
Thyself thou gavest, thy own worth then not knowing,
Or me, to whom thou gavest it, else mistaking;
So thy great gift, upon misprision growing,
Comes home again, on better judgement making.
Thus have I had thee, as a dream doth flatter,
In sleep a king, but, waking, no such matter.

William Shakespeare 1564–1616

To Alexis

Since man with that inconstancy was born,
To love the absent, and the present scorn
Why do we deck, why do we dress
For such short-lived happiness?
Why do we put attraction on,
Since either way 'tis we must be undone?

They fly if honour take our part,
Our virtue drives 'em o'er the field,
We love 'em by too much desert,
And oh! they fly us if we yield.
Ye gods! is there no charm in all the fair
To fix this wild, this faithless wanderer?

Aphra Behn   1640–89

The Forsaken Wife

Methinks 'tis strange you can't afford
One pitying look, one parting word;
HUMANITY claims this as due,
But what's HUMANITY to you?

Cruel Man! I am not blind,
Your infidelity I find;
Your want of Love, my Ruin shows,
My broken Heart, your broken Vows.
Yet maugre all your rigid Hate,
I will be true in spite of Fate;
And one preheminence I'll claim,
To be fore ever still the same.

Show me a Man that dare be TRUE
That dares to suffer what I do;
That can for ever sigh unheard,
And ever love without Regard:
I then will own your Prior Claim
To love, to honour and to fame:
But 'till that time, my Dear, adieu,
I yet SUPERIOR am to you.

Elizabeth Thomas 1675–1731

I Made a House

I made a house of houselessness,
A garden of your going:
And seven tress of seven wounds
You gave me, all unknowing:
I made a feast of golden grief
That you so lordly left me,
I made a bed of all the smiles
Whereof your lip bereft me:
I made a sun of your delay,
Your daily loss, his setting:
I made a wall of all your words
And a lock of your forgetting.

Rose O'Neill late 19th century

Now I Have Nothing

Now I have nothing. Even the joy of loss
Even the dreams I had I now am losing.
Only this thing I know; that you are using
My heart as a stone to bear your foot across …
I am glad I am glad the stone is of your choosing …

Stella Benson 1892–1933

Farewell, Ungrateful Traitor

~

Farewell, ungrateful traitor,
Farewell, my perjured swain,
Let never injured creature
Believe a man again
The pleasure of possessing
Surpasses all expressing,
But 'tis too short a blessing,
And love too long a pain.

'Tis easy to deceive us
In pity of your pain,
But when we love you leave us
To rail at you in vain.
Before we have descried it
There is no bliss beside it,
But she that once has tried it
Will never love again.

The passion you pretended
Was only to obtain,
But when the charm is ended
The charmer you disdain.

Your love by ours we measure
Till we have lost our treasure,
But dying is a pleasure,
When living is a pain.

John Dryden   1631–1700

First Farewell to J.G.

Farewell my dearer half, joy of my heart,
Heaven only knows how loth I am to part:
Whole Months but hours seem, when you are here,
When absent, every Minute is a Year:
Might I but always see thy charming Face,
I'd live on Racks and wish no easier place.
But we must part, your Interest says we must;
Fate, me no longer with such Treasure trust.
I would not tax you with Inconstancy.
Yet Strephon, you are not so kind as I:
No interest, no nor Fate it self has pow'r
To tempt me from the Idol I adore:
But since you needs will go, may Africk be
Kinder to you, that Europe is to me:
May all you meet and every thing you view
Give out such Transport as I met in you.
May no sad thoughts disturb your quiet mind.
Except you'll think of her you left behind.

Ephelia 1678–82

The Gift

What can I give you, my lord, my lover,
You who have given the world to me,
Showed me the light and the joy that cover
The wild sweet earth and the restless sea?

All that I have are gifts of your giving —
If I gave them again, you would find them old,
And your soul would weary of always living
Before the mirror my life would hold.

What shall I give you, my lord, my lover?
The gift that breaks the heart in me:
I bid you awake at dawn and discover
I have gone my way and left you free.

Sara Teasdale 1884–1933

Sonnet

Tell me no more how fair she is,
I have no minde to hear
The story of that distant bliss
I never shall come near:
By sad experience I have found
That her perfection is my wound.

And tell me not how fond I am
To tempt a daring Fate,
From whence no triumph ever came,
But to repent too late:
There is some hope ere long I may
In silence dote my self away.

I ask no pity (Love) from thee,
Nor will thy justice blame,
So that thou wilt not envy mee
The glory of my flame:
Which crowns my heart when ere it dyes,
In that it falls her sacrifice.

Henry King 1592–1669

Like the Touch of Rain

Like the touch of rain she was
On a man's flesh and hair and eyes
When the joy of walking thus
Has taken him by surprise:

With the love of the storm he burns,
He sings, he laughs, well I know how,
But forgets when he returns
As I shall not forget her 'Go now'.

Those two words shut a door
Between me and the blessed rain
That was never shut before
And will not open again.

Edward Thomas 1878–1917

from How Lisa Loved the King

… She watched all day that she might see him
   pass
With knights and ladies; but she said, 'Alas!
Though he should see me, it were all as one
He saw a pigeon sitting on the stone
Of wall or balcony: some coloured spot
His eye just sees, his mind regardeth not.
I have no music-touch that could bring nigh
My love to his soul's hearing. I shall die,
And he will never know who Lisa was –
The trader's child, whose soaring spirit rose
As hedge-born aloe flowers that rarest years
   disclose …'

George Eliot 1819–80

Marriage

No more alone sleeping, no more alone waking
Thy dreams divided, thy prayers in twain;
Thy merry sisters tonight forsaking,
Never shall we see, maiden, again.

Never shall we see, thine eyes glancing,
Flashing with laughter and wild in glee
Under the mistletoe kissing and dancing,
Wantonly free.

There shall come a matron walking sedately,
Low-voiced, gentle, wise in reply.
Tell me, O tell me, can I love her greatly?
All for her sake must the maiden die!

Mary Coleridge 1861–1907

Two Truths

'Darling,' he said, 'I never meant
To hurt you;' and his eyes were wet.
'I would not hurt you for the world:
Am I to blame if I forget?'

'Forgive my selfish tears!' she cried,
'Forgive! I knew that it was not
Because you meant to hurt me, sweet –
I knew it was that you forgot!'

But all the same, deep in her heart
Rankled this thought, and rankles yet, –
'When love is at its best, one loves
So much that he cannot forget.'

Helen Hunt Jackson 1830–85

Once Fondly Lov'd

Once fondly lov'd, and still remember'd dear,
Sweet early object of my youthful vows,
Accept this mark of friendship, warm, sincere –
Friendship! 'tis all cold duty now allows: –

And when you read the simple, artless rhymes,
One friendly sigh for him – he asks no more –
Who distant burns in flaming torrid climes,
Or haply lies beneath th' Atlantic roar.

Robert Burns   1759–96

The Hill

Breathless, we flung us on the windy hill,
Laughed in the sun, and kissed the lovely grass.
You said, 'Through glory and ecstasy we pass;
Wind, sun, and earth remain, the birds sing still,
When we are old, are old …' 'And when we die
All's over that is ours; and life burns on
Through other lovers, other lips,' said I,
'Heart of my heart, our heaven is now, is won!'

'We are Earth's best, that learnt her lesson here.
Life is our cry. We have kept the faith!' we said;
'We shall go down with unreluctant tread
Rose-crowned into the darkness!' … Proud we were,
And laughed, that had such brave true things to say.
— And then you suddenly cried, and turned away.

Rupert Brooke 1887–1915

On the Death of Mrs Bowes

Hail, happy bride, for thou art truly blest!
Three months of rapture, crown'd with endless rest.
Merit like yours was Heav'n's peculiar care,
You lov'd yet tasted happiness sincere.
To you the sweets of love were only shown,
The sure succeeding bitter dregs unknown;
You had not yet the fatal change deplor'd
The tender lover for th'imperious lord;
Nor felt the pain that jealous fondness brings:
Nor felt that coldness from possession springs.
Above your sex, distinguish'd in your fate,
You trusted yet experienc'd no deceit;
Soft were your hours, and wing'd with pleasure flew;
No vain repentance gave a sigh to you:
And if superior bliss Heaven can bestow,
With fellow-angels you enjoy it now.

Lady Mary Wortley Montagu 1689–1762

Not Yet

Time brought me many another friend
That loved me longer.
New love was kind, but in the end
Old love was stronger.

Years come and go. No New Year yet
Hath slain December.
And all that should have cried – 'Forget!'
Cries but – 'Remember!'

Mary Coleridge 1861–1907

The Sad Song

Away delights, go seek some other dwelling
For I must die:
Farewell, false Love, thy tongue is ever telling
Lie after lie.
For ever let me rest now from thy smarts,
Alas, for pity go,
And fire their hearts
That have been hard to thee, mine was not so.

Never again deluding love shall know me
For I will die;
And all those griefs that think to over-grow me,
Shall be as I:
For ever will I sleep, while poor maids cry,
Alas, for pity stay,
And let us die
With thee, men cannot mock us in the clay.

John Fletcher 1579–1625

To Mary: I Sleep With Thee

~

I sleep with thee, and wake with thee,
And yet thou art not there;
I fill my arms with thoughts of thee,
And press the common air.
Thy eyes are gazing upon mine,
When thou art out of sight;
My lips are always touching thine,
At morning, noon, and night.

I think and speak of other things
To keep my mind at rest:
But still to thee my memory clings
Like love in woman's breast.
I hide it from the world's wide eye,
And think and speak contrary;
But soft the wind comes from the sky,
And whispers tales of Mary.

The night wind whispers in my ear,
The moon shines in my face;
A burden still of chilling fear
I find in every place.

The breeze is whispering in the bush,
And the dews fall from the tree,
All sighing on, and will not hush,
Some pleasant tales of thee.

John Clare 1793–1864

May

I cannot tell you how it was;
But this I know: it came to pass
Upon a bright and breezy day
When May was young, ah pleasant May!

As yet the poppies were not born
Between the blades of tender corn
The last eggs had not hatched as yet,
Nor any bird forgone its mate.

I cannot tell you what it was;
But this I know: it did but pass.
It passed away with sunny May,
With all sweet things it passed away,
And left me old, and cold, and grey.

Christina Rossetti 1830–94

A Renouncing of Love

~

Farewell, Love, and all thy laws for ever:
Thy baited hooks shall tangle me no more;
Senec and Plato call me from thy lore,
To perfect wealth my wit for to endeavour.
In blind error when I did perserver,
Thy sharp repulse, that pricketh ay so sore,
Hath taught me to set in trifles no store,
And scape forth, since liberty is lever.
Therefore, farewell: go trouble younger hearts,
And in me claim no more authority;
With idle youth go use thy property,
And thereon spend thy many brittle darts;
For hitherto though I have lost all my time,
Me lusteth no longer rotten boughs to climb.

Sir Thomas Wyatt 1503–42

Farewell Sweet Boy

~

Farewell sweet boy, complain not of my truth;
Thy mother lov'd thee not with more devotion;
For to thy boy's play I gave all my youth,
Young master, I did hope for your promotion.

While some sought honours, princes' thoughts
   observing,
Many woo'd Fame, the child of pain and anguish,
Others judg'd inward good a chief deserving,
I in thy wanton visions joy'd to languish.

I bow'd not to thy image for succession,
Nor bound thy bow to shoot reformed kindness,
Thy plays of hope and fear were my confession,
The spectacles to my life was thy blindness;
But Cupid now farewell, I will go play me,
With thoughts that please me less and less betray me.
                Fulke Greville, Lord Brooke 1554–1628

from Farewell

What should I say,
Since faith is dead,
And truth away
From you is fled?
Should I be led
With doubleness?
Nay, nay, mistress!

I promised you,
And you promised me,
To be as true,
As I would be.
But since I see
Your double heart,
Farewell my part!

Sir Thomas Wyatt 1503–42

from Felix Holt: The Radical

~

This man's metallic; at a sudden blow
His soul rings hard. I cannot lay my palm,
Trembling with life, upon that jointed brass.
I shudder at the cold unanswering touch;
But if it press me in response, I'm bruised.

George Eliot   1819–80

Friendship After Love

After the fierce midsummer all ablaze
Has burned itself to ashes, and expires
In the intensity of its own fires,
There come the mellow, mild, St Martin days
Crowned with the calm of peace, but sad with haze.
So after Love has led us, till he tires
Of his own throes, and torments, and desires,
Comes large-eyed friendship: with a restful gaze,
He beckons us to follow, and across
Cool verdant vales we wander free from care.
Is it a touch of frost lies in the air?
Why are we haunted with a sense of loss?
We do not wish the pain back, or the heat;
And yet, and yet, these days are incomplete.

Ella Wheeler Wilcox 1850–1919

A Farewell

'And if I did, what then?
Are you aggrieved therefore?
The sea hath fish for every man,
And what would you have more?'

Thus did my mistress once
Amaze my mind with doubt;
And popped a question for the nonce,
To beat my brains about.

Whereto I thus replied:
'Each fisherman can wish,
That all the seas at every tide
Were his alone to fish.

'And so did I, in vain,
But since it may not be,
Let such fish there as find the gain,
And leave the loss for me.

'And with such luck and loss
I will content myself,

Till tides of turning time may toss
Such fishers on the shelf.

'And when they stick on sands,
That every man may see,
Then will I laugh and clap my hands,
As they do now at me.'

George Gascoigne 1525–77

Why?

Why did you come, with your enkindled eyes
And mountain-look, across my lower way,
And take the vague dishonour from my day
By luring me from paltry things, to rise
And stand beside you, waiting wistfully
The looming of a larger destiny?

Why did you with strong fingers fling aside
The gates of possibility, and say
With vital voice the words I dream to-day?
Before, I was not much unsatisfied:
But since a god has touched me and departed,
I run through every temple, broken-hearted.

Mary Webb 1881–1927

Sea Love

Tide be runnin' the great world over:
'Twas only last June month I mind that we
Was thinkin' the toss and the call in the breast of the
    lover
So everlastin' as the sea.

Here's the same little fishes that sputter and swim,
Wi' the moon's old glim on the grey, wet sand;
An' him no more to me nor me to him
Than the wind goin' over my hand.

Charlotte Mew 1869–1928

Dead Love

∼

Oh never weep for love that's dead
Since love is seldom true
But changes his fashion from blue to red,
From brightest red to blue,
And love was born to an early death
And is so seldom true.

Then harbour no smile on your bonny face
To win the deepest sigh.
The fairest words on truest lips
Pass on and surely die,
And you will stand alone, my dear,
When wintry winds draw nigh.

Sweet, never weep for what cannot be,
For this God has not given.
If the merest dream of love were true
Then, sweet, we should be in heaven,
And this is only earth, my dear,
Where true love is not given.

Elizabeth Siddal 1834–62

The Way of It

This is the way of it, wide world over,
One is beloved, and one is the lover,
One gives and the other receives.
One lavishes all in a wild emotion,
One offers a smile for a life's devotion,
One hopes and the other believes,
One lies awake in the night to weep,
And the other drifts off in a sweet sound sleep.

One soul is aflame with a godlike passion,
One plays with love in an idler's fashion,
One speaks and the other hears.
One sobs, 'I love you,' and wet eyes show it,
And one laughs lightly, and says, 'I know it,'
With smiles for the other's tears.
One lives for the other and nothing beside,
And the other remembers the world is wide.

This is the way of it, sad earth over,
The heart that breaks is the heart of the lover,
And the other learns to forget.

'For what is the use of endless sorrow?
Though the sun goes down, it will rise to-morrow;
And life is not over yet.'
Oh! I know this truth, if I know no other,
That passionate Love is Pain's own mother.

Ella Wheeler Wilcox 1850–1919

My Life Closed Twice

My life closed twice before its close;
It yet remains to see
If Immortality unveil
A third event to me,

So huge, so hopeless to conceive,
As these that twice befell.
Parting is all we know of heaven,
And all we need of hell.

Emily Dickinson   1830–86

We Who Have Loved

~

We who have loved, alas! may not be friends,
Too faint, or yet too fierce the stifled fire –
A random spark – and lo! our dread desire
Leaps into flame, as though to make amends
For chill, blank days, and with strange fury rends
The dying embers of Love's funeral pyre.
Electric, charged anew, the living wire
A burning message through our torpor sends.
Could we but pledge with loyal hearts and eyes
A friendship worthy of the fair, full past,
Now mutilate, and lost beyond recall,
Then might a Phoenix from its ashes rise
Fit for a soul flight; but we find, aghast,
Love must be nothing if not all in all.

Corinne Roosevelt Robinson late 19th century

'Tis Customary As We Part

~

'Tis customary as we part
A trinket – to confer –
It helps to stimulate the faith
When lovers be afar –

'Tis various – as the various taste –
Clematis – journeying for –
Presents me with a single Curl
Of her Electric Hair –

Emily Dickinson   1830–86

Song

Love a woman? You're an ass!
'Tis a most insipid passion
To choose out for your happiness
The silliest part of God's creation.

Let the porter and the groom,
Things designed for dirty slaves,
Drudge in fair Aurelia's womb
To get supplies for age and graves.

Farewell, woman! I intend
Henceforth every night to sit
With my lewd, well-natured friend,
Drinking to engender wit.

Then give me health, wealth, mirth, and wine,
And, if busy love entrenches,
There's a sweet, soft page of mine
Does the trick worth forty wenches.

John Wilmot, Earl of Rochester 1647–80

Carrefour

O you,
Who came upon me once
Stretched under apple-trees just after bathing,
Why did you not strangle me before speaking
Rather than fill me with the wild white honey of your
    words
And then leave me to the mercy
Of the forest bees?

Amy Lowell 1874–1925

Love Is a Sickness

Love is a sickness full of woes,
All remedies refusing;
A plant that with most cutting grows,
Most barren with best using.
Why so?
More we enjoy it, more it dies;
If not enjoyed, it sighing cries,
Hey ho.
Love is a torment of the mind,
A tempest everlasting;
And Jove hath made it of a kind,
Not well, nor full nor fasting.
Why so?
More we enjoy it, more it dies;
If not enjoyed, it sighing cries,
Hey ho.

Samuel Daniel 1562–1619

Remember

Remember me when I am gone away,
Gone far away into the silent land;
When you can no more hold me by the hand,
Nor I half turn to go yet turning stay.
Remember me when no more day by day
You tell me of our future that you planned:
Only remember me; you understand
It will be late to counsel then or pray.
Yet if you should forget me for a while
And afterwards remember, do not grieve:
For if the darkness and corruption leave
A vestige of the thoughts that once I had,
Better by far you should forget and smile
Than that you should remember and be sad.

Christina Rossetti 1830–94

A Nocturnal Upon St Lucy's Day

'Tis the year's midnight, and it is the day's,
Lucy's, who scarce seven hours herself unmasks,
The sun is spent, and now his flasks
Send forth light squibs, no constant rays;
The world's whole sap is sunk;
The general balm th' hydroptic earth hath drunk,
Whither, as to the bed's-feet, life is shrunk,
Dead and interr'd, yet all these seem to laugh,
Compar'd with me, who am their epitaph.

Study me then, you who shall lovers be
At the next world, that is, at the next spring:
For I am every dead thing,
In whom love wrought new alchemy.
For his art did express
A quintessence even from nothingness,
From dull privations, and lean emptiness:
He ruin'd me, and I am re-begot
Of absence, darkness, death; things which are not.

All others, from all things, draw all that's good,
Life, soul, form, spirit, whence they being have;

I, by love's limbeck, am the grave
Of all, that's nothing. Oft a flood
Have we two wept, and so
Drown'd the whole world, us two; oft did we grow
To be two chaoses, when we did show
Care to ought else; and often absences
Withdrew our souls, and made us carcasses.

But I am by her death, (which word wrongs her)
Of the first nothing, the elixir grown;
Were I a man, that I were one,
I needs must know; I should prefer,
If I were any beast,
Some ends, some means; yea plants, yea stones detest,
And love; all, all some properties invest;
If I an ordinary nothing were,
As shadow, a light, and body must be here.

But I am none; nor will my sun renew.
You lovers, for whose sake the lesser sun
At this time to the Goat is run
To fetch new lust, and give it you,
Enjoy your summer all;

Since she enjoys her long night's festival,
Let me prepare towards her, and let me call
This hour her vigil, and her eve, since this
Both the year's, and the day's deep midnight is.

John Donne   1572–1631

from Don Juan *Cantos 193 and 195*

〜

I loved, I love you, for that love have lost
State, station, heaven, mankind's, my own esteem,
And yet cannot regret what it hath cost,
So dear is still the memory of that dream.
Yet if I name my guilt, 'tis not to boast;
None can deem harshlier of me than I deem.
I trace this scrawl because I cannot rest.
I've nothing to reproach or to request.

You will proceed in beauty and in pride,
Beloved and loving many. All is o'er
For me on earth, except some years to hide
My shame and sorrow deep in my heart's core.
These I could bear, but cannot cast aside
The passion which still rends it as before.
And so farewell — forgive me, love me — no,
That word is idle now, but let it go.

George Gordon, Lord Byron   1788–1824

Brussels and Oxford

~

How first we met do you still remember?
Do you still remember our last adieu?
You were all to me, that sweet September:
Oh, what, I wonder, was I to you?

But I will not ask. I will leave in haze
My thoughts of you, and your thoughts of me;
And will rest content that those sweet fleet days
Are still my tenderest memory.

I often dream how we went together
Mid glimmering leaves and glittering lights,
And watched the twilight Belgian weather
Dying into the starriest nights;

And over our heads the throbbing million
Of bright fires beat, like my heart, on high;
And the music clashed from the lit pavilion,
And we were together, you and I.

But a hollow memory now suffices
For what, last summer, was real and true;

Since here I am by the misty Isis,
And under the fogs of London you.

But what if you, like a swift magician,
Were to change the failing, flowerless year –
Were to make that true that is now a vision
And to bring back summer and Brussels here?

For Fanny, I know, that if you come hither
You will bring with you the time of flowers,
And a breath of the tender Belgian weather,
To Oxford's grey autumnal towers.

And in frost and fog though the late year dies,
Yet the hours again will be warm and fair,
If they meet once more in your dark, deep eyes,
And are meshed again in your golden hair.

William Hurrell Mallock 1849–1923

from Upon the Death of Her Husband

For thee, all thoughts of pleasure I forgo,
For thee, my tears shall never cease to flow;
For thee at once I from the world retire,
To feed in silent shades a hopeless fire.
My bosom all thy image shall retain,
The full impression there shall still remain
As thou has taught my tender heart to prove
The noblest height and elegance of love,
That sacred passion I to thee confine.
My spotless faith shall be for ever thine.

Elizabeth Singer Rowe   1674–1737

The Request of Alexis

Give, give me back that Trifle you despise,
Give me back my Heart, with all its Injuries:
Tho' by your cruelty it wounded be,
The thing is yet of wond'rous Use to me.
A gen'rous Conqueror, when the Battle's won,
Bestows a Charity on the Undone:
If from the well aim'd Stroke no Hope appear,
He kills the Wretch, and shews Compassion there:
But you, Barbarian! keep alive in Pain,
A lasting trophy of Unjust Disdain.

Sarah Dixon   1716–45

On Monsieur's Departure

~

I grieve and dare not show my discontent.
I love and yet am forced to seem to hate,
I do, yet dare not say I ever meant,
I seem stark mute yet inwardly do prate.
I am and not, I freeze and yet am burned
Since from myself my other self I turned.

My care is like my shadow in the sun,
Follows me flying, flies when I pursue it,
Stands and lies by me, doth what I have done
His too familiar care doth make me rue it.
No means I find to rid him from my breast,
Till by the end of things it be supprest.

Some gentler passions slide into my mind
For I am soft and made of melting snow;
Or be more cruel, love, and so be kind.
Let me or float or sink, be high or low.
Or let me live with some more sweet content,
Or die and so forget what love ere meant.

Queen Elizabeth I 1533–1603

Love and Friendship

Love is like the wild rose-briar,
Friendship like the holly tree –
The holly is dark when the rose-briar blooms
But which will bloom most constantly?

The wild rose-briar is sweet in spring,
Its summer blossoms scent the air;
Yet wait till winter comes again
And who will call the wild-briar fair?

Then scorn the silly rose-wreath now
And deck thee with the holly's sheen,
That when December blights thy brow
He still may leave thy garland green.

Emily Brontë   1818–48

Vitae Summa Brevis

They are not long, the weeping and the laughter,
Love and desire and hate:
I think they have no portion in us after
We pass the gate.

They are not long, the days of wine and roses:
Out of a misty dream
Our path emerges for a while, then closes
Within a dream.

Ernest Dowson   1867–1900

Written Beneath a Picture

Dear object of defeated care!
Though now of Love and thee bereft,
To reconcile me with despair
Thine image and my tears are left.

'Tis said with Sorrow Time can cope;
But this I feel can ne'er be true:
For by this death-blow of my Hope
My Memory immortal grew.
George Gordon, Lord Byron   1788–1824

At the Mid Hour of Night

~

At the mid hour of night, when stars are weeping, I fly
To the lone vale we loved, when life shone warm in
  thine eye;
And I think that, if spirits can steal from the region
  so fair
To revisit past scenes of delight, thou wilt come to me
  there,
And tell me our love is remembered even in the sky.

Then I sing the wild song it once was such rapture to
  hear,
When our voices commingling breathed like one on
  the ear;
And as Echo far off through the vale my sad orison
  rolls,
I think O my love! 'tis thy voice from the Kingdom of
  Souls
Faintly answering still the notes that once were so
  dear.

Thomas Moore 1779–1852

False Though She Be

False though she be to me and love,
I'll ne'er pursue revenge;
For still the charmer I approve
Though I deplore her change.

In hours of bliss we oft have met:
They could not always last;
And though the present I regret,
I'm grateful for the past.

William Congreve 1670–1729

Song

When lovely woman stoops to folly,
And finds too late that men betray,
What charm can soothe her melancholy,
What art can wash her guilt away?

The only art her guilt to cover,
To hide her shame from every eye,
To give repentance to her lover,
And wring his bosom – is to die.

Oliver Goldsmith 1730–74

On His Dead Wife

~

Methought I saw my late espoused saint
Brought to me like Alcestis from the grave,
Whom Jove's great son to her glad husband gave,
Rescued from death by force, though pale and faint.
Mine, as whom washed from spot of childbed taint
Purification in the old Law did save,
And such as yet once more I trust to have
Full sight of her in heaven without restraint,
Came vested all in white, pure as her mind.
Her face was veiled, yet to my fancied sight
Love, sweetness, goodness, in her person shined
So clear as in no face with more delight,
But O as to embrace me she inclined,
I waked, she fled, and day brought back my night.

John Milton 1608–74

from A Leave Taking

Let us go hence, my songs; she will not hear.
Let us go hence together without fear;
Keep silence now, for singing-time is over,
And over all old things and all things dear
She loves not you nor me as we all love her.
Yea, though we sang as angels in her ear,
She would not hear.

Algernon Swinburne 1837–1909